INTELLIGENCE GATHERING

Front Line HUMINT Considerations

Orlando "Andy" Wilson

Orlando "Andy" Wilson

"Nobody can guard your secrets better than you, so do not blame anyone for revealing your secrets because you could not hide them yourself. Your secret is your prisoner, which if let loose it will make you its prisoner."
Imam Ali (AS)

CONTENTS

Title Page

Copyright

Dedication

THE BASICS 1

INTELLIGENCE 8

SECRECY 11

INTELLIGENCE GATHERING 15

COUNTER-SURVEILLANCE 29

COVERT COMMUNICATIONS GUIDE 40

ELECTRONIC SURVEILLANCE 53

BUGGING CONSIDERATIONS 58

PHOTOGRAPHY 63

ATTENDING MEETINGS 69

KIDNAP, ROBBERY, & RAPE DRUGS 73

THE SEX BUSINESS – A GATEWAY TO BLACKMAIL & EXTORTION 76

SEXTORTION – ONLINE EXTORTION 83

INTERVIEWS & DEBRIEFS 85

BEING ARRESTED 92

INTERROGATION 97

ESCAPE & EVASION 103

ORLANDO "ANDY" WILSON   115

OTHER BOOKS BY ORLANDO   117

THE BASICS

Years ago, a client asked me to do some research on a gentleman in one of the former Soviet Republics. The client had a major issue with this person, who happened to move in very dubious circles. The client, who was very credible and established, said to me he could get this gentleman killed, but this would not worry him as such things were part of the criminal world he existed in.

The client told me he wanted to destroy this gentleman's reputation, ruin his legitimate business and legally seize his assets. The client knew this gentleman's reputation and assets were worth more to him than his life. To achieve his objective the client needed accurate intelligence on his target. Intelligence is power, it can make someone or break them, literally.

I think since human beings first learned how to talk, they have been spying and telling tails on each other. The only thing that has changed with intelligence gathering from the time Sun Tzu wrote his classic book "The Art of War" in the 5th Century BC and today is the technological advancements that only really started to develop in the 20th century. The basics of tradecraft, personal security, and recruiting informants, etc. are still very similar if not the same as in the times of Sun Tzu and earlier.

Most of the things I talk about in this book are double-sided; you can use the techniques to target others, but they can also be used to target you. If you're involved in serious investigative or intelligence work, you must always be on the watch out for others targeting you in one way or the other.

The information and techniques I talk about in this book are simple, most are just common sense, but they will give you and insight into the skills and mindset required for HUMINT and counterintelligence operations. Operationally you must always keep things as simple as possible, the more complicated things are, the more that can go wrong. Bullshit can baffle brains and many people seem to think if they over-complicate something it makes them seem intelligent and gives them more content to show a client, etc. That's all good if you're a bullshiter dealing with bullshit clients, but if you're dealing with serious clients and situations always keep things as simple, factual and direct as possible. Believe me, things can get very complicated, very quickly even with the best planned and apparently simple operations, so avoid the bullshit.

In the intelligence and investigations world, people always talk about keeping a low profile, which you should always try to do to the best of your ability. The issue arises when you run a business providing investigations, research or surveillance services. You need to advertise your services and network or else you won't have any clients. Working out how to layer your business, keep a low profile and at the same time market yourself needs to be part of your business plan and protocols.

These days if you're running a legitimate business you have to be on record somewhere, at a basic level, your company registration or your professional licenses at least. In most countries, information on company registration and professional licenses is publicly available which can compromise your personal security to start with. Where legal, always use virtual offices, addresses and phone numbers for your company's registration and licenses.

Below are just some very basic tips I give people who are dealing with debt collectors. I advise everyone who owns a business to think about layering their business and assets if for no other reason than these days it's very easy to get sued. Layering your business and assets will help you understand how such procedures and protocols work. As I said, most of the information in this book is double-sided, and asset locations are very much part of the intelligence business.

• Own Nothing, transfer the ownership of your home, cars and valuable possessions to someone you trust or to a corporation.

• Set up a corporation with other trusted partners so the company bank accounts and assets cannot be seen as your personal bank accounts.

• If your corporation is going under then sell off its assets and transfer the registered corporate office address to a virtual office or mailbox and the phone numbers to a voice mail.

• If you're going into debt sell your cars and possessions to trusted friends or family and retain rights of use.

• Always research your local laws on company protection of assets, debt and debt collection.

I am regularly asked by people how they can get passports in different names and set up new identities for themselves. The truthful answer is that legally you can't. If you're stupid enough to try to use fake government-issued identification documents, you can end up in a lot of trouble. Making private company or press ID's with fake names on them is not an issue but buying fake driving licenses and passports is illegal.

In many places fake and stolen passports, driving licenses and government papers are for sale if you know the right people or find the right websites and don't get scammed. I know of one idiot who decided to buy a fake passport and attempted to travel on it. He got on the plane without problems, but when his papers were checked by the immigration officers from the country he arrived in, they wanted to know why he had a passport belonging to someone that had been murdered in an EU country about 6 months before.

To make this wannabee James Bond's situation even worse he had mailed his own original passport back to his country, so he was arrested for traveling on fake documents and initially connected to a murder. He ended up serving 6 months in prison and then deported back to his own country, where the cops were waiting to have a chat with him also.

One issue these days for investigators, especially when traveling, is having your computers and phones checked by airport security or the police. In a lot of countries not unlocking your computers or phones to be inspected by the police is a criminal offense. I recommend you always comply with the laws of the countries you are in, just remove anything from your computers and phones you don't want others to see.

There are many ways of sending sensitive investigation notes and reports these days. Keeping such items on your electronic devices while going through airport security or in sensitive locations is very dangerous and stupid. A simple technique is to upload sensitive information to a cloud app or email server and then take the app off your phone after the upload. When you need to access the information again just reinstall the app and log into your account.

It's easy and affordable to buy smartphones and SIM cards in most places in the world today. For operational phones buy specific phones for that operation and only keep information and apps on them that are relevant. After the operation, the phone can be presented as evidence, stored as part of the case file or disassembled and destroyed.

If you're running a professional business you must keep things legal, every element of an operation needs to be assessed to ensure it is legal in the locations that you're running it. If you're collecting evidence that is going to be used in court, you must ensure it's collected within the guidelines for admissible evidence for that court and legal system.

I have been involved in the security and investigation industry internationally since leaving the British Army in 1993 and things have changed dramatically since then... As I said earlier the basic physical tactics, techniques and procedures have remained more or less the same but, with the development of the internet communications, logistics and networking are in a completely different world. Sadly, though, many are still stuck in the 1990s.

One of the first large investigations I completed when I started working for myself in the mid-90s was to locate a fishing trawler in the far East of Russia. This entailed getting contacts to 1. Locate the vessel 2. Take and develop photos 3. Send to Moscow 4. Fax me the photos and report from Moscow 5. Originals were sent to me via FedEx 6. Forwarded to the client. This job took about 3 weeks if I remember correctly. These days as soon as the vessel was located, we could stream real-time video to the client via a smartphone...

I find it funny how many people seeking work, and quite a few working, in the specialist security or investigations industry have completed many tactical or weapons courses and may be licensed in numerous locations but are still lacking the basic soft skills required to be able to complete the most basic tasks... I class these basic skills as life skills that apply to virtually everyone, especially those who work for themselves.

These skills include:

• Must be able to use a computer or smartphone

• Must be able to use various messenger apps

• Must be able to write a report

• Must be able to take viewable photos and video

• Must be able to plan a route and use maps, physical & digital

• Must be able to get from one location to another on time, internationally

• Must be able to book flights, hotels and cars internationally

• Must be able to send and receive money internationally

You might be the best shot or hardest puncher in the world but if you can't communicate or get from point A to B without drama, you're a waste of space. Not being able to send funds internationally can lead to delays in tasks being completed or canceled.

One thing I did not list which is an essential skill is to know how to research and set up companies in various locations. For many operations, it helps if your targets think the people they are talking to are in different countries. You can legally and with minimal cost, set up registered companies, virtual offices, phone numbers in numerous countries that can give credibility to any fake websites or social media accounts you might have set up for the operation.

Many times, I have set up jobs where the fraudsters we were looking into and targeting thought they were dealing with companies and people in different countries, when in fact we were in the same city and we had people standing behind them most mornings when they were buying their coffee and doughnuts.

Personal security is something you must take extremely seriously especially if you start investigating and researching corrupt officials and criminals. You must understand that if you are under an active threat, it will also apply to your family, friends and business partners. You need to ensure that the people in your inner circle understand they need to be vigilant for security threats and suspicious of approaching strangers.

Something as simple as bringing someone into your home can cause problems as they will have access to your computers, phones, records, personal space and security protocols. You need to be very careful with personal and professional relationships and should never discuss investigations, operations or targets with people that don't need to know, especially lovers, spouses and family. They can interpret those conversations as casual chats that they can repeat to their bored friends or other family members.

Remember, loyalty is bought, and no-one owes you anything. People will stab you in the back and betray you if it's worth their while, with little concern for the issues or consequences you or your family will have to deal with. If you think this is a harsh outlook, then remember what I said earlier "Most of the things in this book are double-sided".

Your job, or the job you want, involves you buying the loyalty and gaining the trust of people whom you will betray to achieve your objectives, without concern for the issues and consequences they might have to deal with due to your actions. And that's why you're reading this book!

Orlando Wilson

April 2020

INTELLIGENCE

Intelligence is the information we obtain on a target or threat in order to locate them, gain information on their operations and to predict their future actions. Accurate intelligence is not only essential in all security and counter-insurgency operations but also in the corporate world where companies need to know what their competitors are developing and planning.

An easy way to illustrate the importance of intelligence and counterintelligence is this simple example; randomly pick someone online or someone you know and say to yourself "I'm going to kill this person". They are defenseless as they do not even know you are targeting them, if they even know you exist. You can start profiling the target and making your plans for the assassination while they are completely oblivious.

Intelligence and counterintelligence are two sides of the same coin. You cannot expect to be able to source intelligence unless you are alert for others targeting you. Egos and arrogance get people killed. Those who think they know everything and are untouchable are usually the easiest to bring crashing down. Especially if those targeting them are professional, ruthless and unconventional.

There are various means of gathering intelligence but no matter where the information is coming from it needs to be verified and crosschecked to ensure its accuracy and that it is not disinformation provided intentionally. If information and leads are being provided from reliable sources, then every little detail needs to be taken into consideration. One single fact, however apparently insignificant, can open the doors that lead you to your target.

Intelligence Gathering Can Roughly Be Divided Into Three Areas

• **Surveillance:** This can include physically following a target, watching the target's home or office, hacking telephones and computers to intercept messages, monitor web traffic and movements, etc.

• **Research and Analysis:** Useful information can be found from online news reports, photos, social media, newspapers, radio and trade magazines, etc.

• **Informants and Espionage:** The placing or recruiting of agents and informants with access to the target and their organization can be difficult, time-consuming and dangerous for all involved, but can give you access to the target's plans, documents, networks and the ability to influence or misdirect their activities and goals.

Some of the basic tasks of intelligence operations are to:

• Locate criminal and hostile targets.

• Identify criminal and hostile activities.

• Identify the structure, plans and goals of an organization or corporation

• Identify and penetrate an organization or corporation

• Obtain information about an area and its population.

The Intelligence Cycle

The intelligence Cycle is a set of simple bullet points that are used by intelligence agencies to effectively structure their operations.

• **Direction:** You need to know the objectives and goals for every operation be it short or long term.

• **Collection:** You need to have a plan for how you will collect the required information; open-source, informants, surveillance, hacking, etc.

• **Processing:** Once your collection operation starts to deliver information it needs to be checked for accuracy and relevance.

• **Analysis:** When you have accurate and reliable information or leads you need to assess what it actually identifies, and how the information can be used.

• **Dissemination:** How will you use the information and who will be informed of your findings.

• **Feedback:** Once your reports have been distributed you will need to wait to see what feedback is given from your clients or the like. Be prepared to defend your finding especially if they are controversial or go against what the client expected to be discovered.

The type of information that will be of use to you will depend on the type of operations that you are conducting. You need to clearly define why you are running your operation and what the required end-results are. Only then you can collate the relevant information required to achieve your goals and start to dismiss false leads, disinformation and irrelevant information.

SECRECY

Nothing is as important professionally or personally as secrecy. All your security, operational or business plans and preparations will be worthless if the bad guys know them. If you cannot protect yourself there is no way you can protect others or work in any potential hostile environments.

Good personal and operational security begins with a clear understanding of what kind of information the criminals or terrorists will be trying to learn about you, your family, business or operations.

Governments must keep secret their diplomatic alliances, secret treaties and military strategies, etc. Although a government may suffer a great loss because of poor security, it is hard to imagine today a situation where a nation's defenses could be completely overwhelmed by a single security leak. However, that is not the case with a small-scale operation.

A company might be ruined as the result of a single security leak. A family might be ambushed and kidnapped because a single piece of information was found out by the criminals, such as a home address, security procedures, routes a child takes to school or their travel itinerary.

Things That Should Be Kept Secret And Restricted

• Addresses and identity of individual employees, their families or close friends.

• Security plans and methods of operation.

• Transportation capabilities.

- Sources of supplies.

- Available backup.

- Location of hideouts and safe houses, etc.

- Codes, signals, passwords, and lines of communications.

Good personal security is a must, good team security begins with good personal security. If a person is living or traveling under their own name, they must keep information about their occupation and activities limited to those who need to know only. There is no one more completely defenseless than the individual whose personal security has been compromised.

Personal security is a 24/7 job, to some, it comes almost instinctively but others can find it very hard to develop. An individual's habits and personality will have a considerable effect on their attitude towards personal security. Some people will just never get it and it can be a liability. Such people should not be allowed access to sensitive information or taken to high-risk locations.

The Basic Principals Of Security

- **Deception:** Deception is essential to the success of all security or investigative operations; always have a cover story and be ready with credible explanations as to who you are, what you're doing and why you are doing it.

- **Avoiding attention:** One way for any individual or organization to seriously compromise their security is to attract attention. Always keep a low profile and remember that if people don't know what you are doing, they cannot counteract you.

- **Self-discipline:** Everyone must abide by the rules. If anyone disregards the rules of the security program, they could jeopardize the personal security of all involved.

- **The program:** A security program must be outlined and made clear to all personnel. Everyone must be briefed, trained and willing to work within the program.

- **Continual inspection:** The biggest thieves are usually those trusted with the largest responsibilities- they have access to assets or information worth stealing. The conscientious person with the flawless record can easily deviate by their own accord or with the pressure of a little blackmail. People change and so does the importance they place on their own security; given time people will relax. This is why there is a need for everyone to be constantly inspected.

- **Fluid change:** This is best illustrated by frequent changes of meeting places, routes and operational procedures to keep the criminals guessing. This principle is necessary because, if given enough time, professional criminals can crack the security of any organization. So, old security measures must be constantly and fluidly replaced and updated.

- **Action:** If someone is not capable of obeying the security program they will need to be disciplined, they should not be trusted or only trusted with information or tasks that will not jeopardize anyone else.

You will not have a security program by following only one or more of these principles, all must be followed, and you must remain alert 24/7.

Basic Counterintelligence

Basic counterintelligence increases the security of all operations and the chances of surprise in offensive operations. Your security program, even if it is for yourself, should be developed to prevent the leaking of information, or situations where criminals can extract information from you or your business.

You could initially be trying to find criminal sympathizers already within your operation; this could be your locally recruited secretary or attorney. If you detect a sympathizer within your operation what are you going to do, fire them or feed them false information? You should also consider why they sympathize with the criminals: is it for money or are they being threatened. Counterintelligence can be broken down in to two practices, denial and detection operations.

Basic denial operations may include:

• Thoroughly brief everyone on how the criminals will try to get information on you, your personnel and your operation.

• Place a high emphasis on the security of information. People must understand the need to keep things on a "need to know" basis and not to talk about confidential topics in public.

• Make sure all papers, old computers and communication devices, etc. are properly disposed of.

• Employees should be briefed on the gyms, cafés, bars, clubs and other venues that are safe to frequent socially and those that are not.

Basic detection operations may include:

• Background investigations must be done on all employees, especially locals who have access to confidential information.

• Make maximum use of CCTV, covert cameras for detection and overt cameras for deterrence.

• Monitor your staff's communications including e-mail, web activity and telephone calls, etc.

• Put any staff members acting suspiciously or who seem to be living beyond their means under investigation and surveillance.

These are just some basic considerations, but they can turn your security program into something that would make it extremely difficult for the bad guys to gain information on you. If they cannot get any information on you it makes their job targeting you a lot harder. Hopefully, so hard they'll go and do what we want them to do, find an easier target of which there are plenty.

INTELLIGENCE GATHERING

I wrote the below notes on intelligence gathering a few years ago for a project I was dealing with in West Africa. These notes highlight basic intelligence gathering techniques that can be used against criminals and terrorists but can also be used against you.

A lot of time those engaged in counter-terrorism and organized crime operations do not take adequate counterintelligence precautions to protect themselves, their assets or the operations they are working on. As you read through this chapter think about how you could be targeted and what you could do to prevent information leaks.

The best way to learn how to defend something is to learn how to attack it. So, from a training perspective try targeting others you know with some of the techniques I have listed here. I think you will be surprised to see how vulnerable the vast majority of people are, just try to ensure you're not one of them!

Human Intelligence Gathering

Good intelligence is the most important element in all counter-insurgency (COIN) operations. Your goal is to build an accurate picture of the terrorists' and criminals' network, their identities, safe houses, capabilities, contacts, sources of supplies and finances, etc. Below are a few considerations on how to gain intelligence on terrorist or criminal organizations.

False Intelligence

You must always verify all the information you intercept or is supplied to you, never take things at face value. Unverified information needs to be treated as unreliable or with great caution even if the source is reliable, as they could have been compromised. Sources need to be rated according to their reliability, which can only be done over time. They might have gotten lucky and provided a solid lead once but everything after that one gem still needs to be verified.

When information is supplied, think what was the reason the source supplied it, what was their incentive to supply the information? Are they looking for payment, are they trying to discredit an opponent or lead you into a trap, etc.? All this needs to be analyzed. Over time a source's reliability and value should become clear, and they should be rewarded likewise or no longer used unless it's to spread disinformation.

Disinformation is something that can be used either against you or in your favor. The terrorists and criminals can feed you false information to lead you off their trail or into ambushes, etc. That is why all information needs to be verified. If staging an operation based on a source's information, then precautions need to be taken at all stages of the operations to avoid compromise or ambush. You can also use disinformation to lure the terrorists into arrest or ambush locations and to spread confusion or conflicts within their organization, etc.

These days with social media it's easy to spread disinformation and to use fake profiles to entrap people. From a defensive perspective, you can tag yourself and post photos from locations you're nowhere near to or locations you have under surveillance to see if anyone comes looking for you. From the offensive perspective, setting up fake social media or dating profiles to approach or attract those you're targeting is a basic and proven tactic and a favorite for scammers and identity thieves.

Always be very cautious when analyzing any intelligence that has been supplied to you. Always use your imagination to the max when looking to spread disinformation and don't be afraid to play dirty. If your target's wife receives a message from her husband's pregnant girlfriend that can instigate conflict and discourse, this can possibly get the wife to give up the target's location, or bring the target out into the open to smooth things over with his disgruntled wife, etc. Use your imagination...

Media & Social Media

You should monitor all media sources such as printed newspapers, social media and the internet for interviews, stories and photos on your target. These days the emphasis is placed on social media but in many developing countries local printed newspapers and radio are the main sources of news and current affairs and should be monitored.

Any journalists who are writing stories about the terrorist or criminal organizations should be monitored and the setting up of pseudo media operations offering interview opportunities to the terrorist or criminals and their supporters should be considered.

Communications

Once a terrorist or criminal suspect or supporter has been identified you should target their communications. All terrorist and criminal organizations need to be able to communicate internally within their organization and externally with family members, sources of supplies, etc. Interception of the target's lines of communication is an excellent source of valuable intelligence. Remember, if you cannot target the person you are looking for directly then target those whom you suspect they are dealing with and wait for him or her to communicate with them.

• **Mail**: People still use snail mail and written messages can be intercepted, then read or modified to your needs.

• **Landline Phones:** It may come as a shock to many people these days, but landline phones are still used, and payphones can still be found. Landlines are easy to bug with commercially available equipment. If the terrorists or criminals are using payphones, you want to identify any patterns of use via the numbers they are using, then locate and bug the phones as well as put them under remote camera or physical surveillance if your resources and budget allow.

• **Mobile Phones:** If you can access a target's mobile phone you will have access to their location, network and communications. Access can be gained by sending trojan applications, by having sources close to the target install spyware or by gifting new phones, again through sources close to the target. Where budgets allow IMSI-catchers (stingers) should be acquired and employed. IMSI-catchers are devices that are used for intercepting mobile phone traffic and tracking the location and data of mobile phone users. They are expensive and are officially only available to military and law enforcement agencies but are available on the black market. Warning: Such devices are in the hands of terrorist and criminal organizations as they are bought from or through corrupt officials who have access to the equipment or required end-user certificates.

• **Email & Computers:** Unsecured computers and Wi-Fi connections can give you access to a supply of constant and up to date information. As with mobile phones, access can be gained through trojan applications, having sources install spyware, hacking operations or by getting hold of account passwords.

• **Radios:** Most commercial walkie-talkie and CB radio signals can be intercepted with radio scanners. In remote areas a radio scanner on permanent scan will pick up all the radio communications being sent in the area. In urban areas there can be issues with interference due to the number of signals which can be an advantage for the terrorists and criminals but make it difficult for those targeting them.

Family And Friends

Most people only communicate with a small group of family, friends and associates. If you are targeting someone, their friends and family can generally lead you to them. Usually, if someone is OTR (On The Run) or in hiding, it is only a matter of time before they contact their family or known friends, etc.

• The mail, phones, computers and social media of the target's family and associates can be monitored.

• The family and associates can be placed under physical or remote surveillance to see if they contact the target, their associates or are buying supplies for the target.

• The business and home addresses of the target's family and associates can be put under surveillance, mail and phone lines monitored and listening devices placed within the buildings. Also, monitor the electricity or water bills for the building. If the electricity, water usage or food deliveries, etc. increase suddenly, or are in excess for the known occupants, there could possibly be someone hiding in the building.

• Cars of the target's family and associates can be fitted with tracking and listening devices.

Locals And Neighbors

Locals and neighbors of the target, their family and associates can prove to be good sources of intelligence. Send a socially skilled operative to speak with them paying special attention to anyone who shows a dislike for the target, their family and associates. Local children can also provide information on activity in the area and might not be as guarded and keener to talk than adults.

Documents

Any seized or acquired papers need to be analyzed for forensics as well as the information they contain. Even the smallest pieces of paperwork should not be overlooked, such as shopping receipts that show locations, dates and times, etc. that can be acquired from the target or their family's garbage, etc.

Sources Of Supplies

All terrorist and criminal organizations need to be supplied with weapons, ammunition, food, medical equipment, gasoline and cash, etc. For example, mobile phones need SIM cards and the accounts need to be topped up with funds, so where and how are the terrorist or criminals doing this? Once sources are identified they can then be monitored, and the supplies tracked to the target or modified before delivery.

Routes Or Areas Frequented

Suspected routes used and locations frequented for social activity, etc. by the target should be monitored or ambushed. If the target is spotted, they can be followed or arrested, etc. as can their known associates.

If you're sending people to hang out in cafés, bars or clubs frequented by your targets ensure they fit in with the other people in that location. A rigid former career soldier in his 40's will not fit in with an under 25 crowd at a pool party, unless he's pretending to be someone's sugar daddy. If you're sending people into bars make sure they have some tolerance for alcohol and won't be drunk, acting stupid and talking too much after a few beers. If you're sending people into brothels or strip bars make sure they have some life experience and won't be acting like terrified virgins or excited adolescents when they see a naked woman.

Rewards

Rewards can be offered for information on the targets. All information would need to be verified as you can expect a large amount of bogus information, if not outright disinformation, to be called in. Rewards need to be paid if the information supplied proves to be accurate. Not paying rewards would lead to the program losing its credibility very quickly.

Spying Operations

Where possible, a network of informers (sources) should be established. You should seek to recruit people who could have information on the targets or are close to them. Methods of recruitment for sources varies greatly from person to person and depends a lot on their personality and reason for giving up information on the target. Our initial phase is to find people who have a grudge against the target; they could be owed money, be ex-lovers, etc. They could possibly still be in contact with the target or be able to establish communications because they are seeking revenge or compensation in return for cooperating.

The second group of potential recruits would be those who under normal circumstances would not be considered sources of information. These are people who would need to be persuaded to provide information on the targets. If you believe someone could provide you with information and be a semi-reliable source, you will need to compile a lifestyle check on the person and identify anything that could be used against them. Such as debts, vices (sex, drug or alcohol use, gambling, etc.), extramarital affairs, criminal activity, etc. that they would not want to become public knowledge and, would be willing to provide information on the target to prevent this from happening. A little pressure can sometimes work wonders and useful information and actions should always be rewarded.

Sources and informants need to understand that they should not let anyone know they are working for or with you. I know of one situation in the US where a businessman had a falling out with someone who happened to be an auxiliary cop, which means they made donations to a police department to be given a police badge.

The businessman was approached by the local police out of the blue for bullshit reasons on numerous occasions and a few days after every incident the auxiliary cop always tried to contact the businessman, even though he had blocked his known phone numbers and social media accounts.

We take it the auxiliary cop was giving bullshit reports to his cop buddies so they would fuck with the businessman. The reason the auxiliary cop was trying to contact the businessman was part of his egotistical power trip: he wanted to show the businessman he could fuck with him. You need to ensure the people you recruit are not prone to going on power trips or spending sprees with any cash you give them as they can end up compromising whole operations and getting themselves and others killed.

Everyone in your network should be offered some form of compensation. If you identify a potential source has debts, then money could be the only incentive they need to provide information on the target. Any exchanges of cash or assets with sources need to be videoed and could be used in the future if the source becomes uncooperative.

Official records need to be kept on all sources and informants, but in high-risk environments, where your communications devices and records could be compromised you need to be very careful. Code names need to be allocated for sources and informants so they cannot be identified by 3rd parties and in high-risk environments their personal photos and details need to be kept off record. Source records can include:

• Name, photograph, and physical description of the source.

• Home and business addresses

• Details of family

• Details of lovers and extramarital affairs

• Details of business partners

- Source's motivation for providing information
- How the source was developed
- Area in which the source can obtain information
- Source's connections with criminal or terrorist organizations
- Method by which the source can be contacted
- Record of payments or other remuneration
- Productivity and reliability of the source.

Source Security

The identities of your sources must be kept on a "need to know" basis, code names need to be allocated and used as soon as a potential source is identified. The personal security of the source and their family needs to be considered always. If a source is compromised, they need to be informed and if possible, relocated ASAP.

If a source is killed or kidnapped, it can lead to fear in other sources who may become uncooperative. It would be good operational procedure for a terrorist group to routinely punish or execute suspected informants within their organizations. Even if those executed were innocent it would serve as a severe warning to those considering becoming informants.

If people know they are safe and will be looked after, they will be more productive. All files and evidence on sources need to be kept secure, encrypted and quickly disposable. That being said, security concerns for a source always need to be evaluated and should never inhibit the success of an operation.

The Placing Of Undercover Operatives

This is a situation where one of your operatives tries to infiltrate the terrorist or criminal organization. Your operative would need to appear to be a sympathizer to the terrorist cause and have similar interests to those he or she is seeking to become friends with.

When a suitable terrorist or one of their supporters is identified, the operative would try to strike up a relationship with them. The initial approach would not be about the terrorist's cause but should be about a common interest such as sports, food, dating, etc. You would need to compile a lifestyle check on the target for the operative and identify anything that could assist them in building a relationship with the target.

A suitable time and location for this first approach would need to be determined, this is when things can get off to a good start or no start at all. Over time it would be the operative's job to win the confidence of their target. The path the relationship takes will determine how the target could be used. If they are loyal to their cause they should hopefully be able to supply valuable information. If they are disgruntled with their cause they could be turned or guided to cause friction within the terrorist or criminal organization.

How involved the operative will become with the target and the terrorist or criminal organizations will depend on the situation and their safety. If an operative is left in place dealing with the terrorists or criminals for an extended period there is a chance, they themselves could turn to the terrorist or criminal cause. The operative's mental wellbeing needs to be closely monitored and they should be given continuous reassurance and support.

Honey Traps

Honey Traps are a spy and criminal tactic that has been around for as long as humans have, but still people, usually men, end up getting entrapped, extorted, kidnapped or murdered. The trap is simple, usually a woman provides or promises a man sexual favors used to blackmail him or to lure him to a location to be killed or kidnapped, etc... The threat is that prevalent that in May 2018 the British Security Service MI5 distributed the "The Smart Traveler" booklet to help protect UK businessmen from honey traps, substance misuse and other entrapment tactics while doing business abroad.

Now think about it: which of the guys you know would say "NO" to an afternoon of sexual games with two attractive young women if you offered it as a gift? Not many, I expect, well I know for a fact... Such a gift can be easily arranged. You just need two female (or male) prostitutes, a hotel room or better still an apartment or an Airbnb these days. Apartments give more privacy and can be easier to rig cameras in... Then the target's afternoon of sexual ecstasy will quickly turn into a nightmare for their foreseeable future...

Honey traps happen all the time and have since men's dicks controlled their brains, so forever. At the low end of the scale, the hot chick will promise a night of debauchery but will just take her target to a shady hotel room or apartment where they can be beaten, robbed and maybe raped by her waiting accomplices. At a higher level, a more intricate honey trap can go on for an extended period of time until the target believes it's some form of relationship, of course, the sex - the more deviant the better - would be videoed and then used to blackmail them for business favors or hard currency.

A common criminal tactic is to pimp out a girl or boy who looks of the legal consenting age for sex and then claim after the sex has taken place, they are underage. That way they have a lot of leverage on the unfortunate and stupid gent who has, unknowingly, possibly committed a serious criminal act: sex with a minor.

Psychological Operations

In simple terms psychological operations are media campaigns and other such actions to impact the opinions, emotions, attitudes, and behavior of hostile, neutral, or friendly groups to support the achievement of your desired objectives. Within counter-criminal and terrorist operations properly employed psychological operations can help you gain support and promote a favorable image of your organization or your clients and at the same time discredit your opponents.

You need to consider who are the audiences that you need to influence and tailor the information that is given to them to ensure they respond as required. This is where accurate intelligence combined with disinformation can be packaged and distributed to ensure it has the maximum effect. Your audiences can include:

• Your opponents: Work out a campaign to discredit and isolate them from their family, friends and supporters.

• Those supporting your opponents: Highlight betrayals and failures that can cause infighting and division.

• Those who are supporting you or your clients: Promote any injustices you have suffered and how you're working to rectify the wrongs done to you, your associates and the community.

• Those who are neutral: You need to convince this group that your actions or those of your clients are justified and that you have been victimized. Also, highlight the negative actions and crimes of your opponents.

Psychological operations when properly planned can have a devastating effect on the public image and reputation of an individual or organization. These days what the public views on social media can prove to be someone's judge, jury and executioner.

Dissemination

Once you have the information, photos or evidence you were after you have to work out and plan how you are going to use it. These days with social media it's easy to promote stories and videos to a vast audience very quickly and affordably. It does not take much time or skill to set up social media accounts to host stories, photos, videos that can then be promoted to the audiences you want.

For non-virtual and real-world applications, understanding people's circumstances and thought processes can help you solve a multitude of problems legally and discreetly. I once helped an overtly happily married client that was being extorted by a ghetto prostitute he invited to his house when his wife and kids were away for the weekend.

To cut a long story short, after making it obvious in the neighborhood where this young lady lived that we were looking for her and wanted a chat, for some reason she did not want to talk to me... So, I ended up calling her mobile number that I had from day one. Of course, she knew I was the guy that was looking for her and she offered to meet me and to bring her people with all their guns, which was an expected response.

I asked her a simple question, "What would the people in your neighborhood do if they found out you just ripped someone off for $50,000?". That one question stopped the client being extorted and the girl, stopped contacting him. She knew what the people in her neighborhood would do and so did I. Everything my associates I had done was legal, and we solved the problem, because we had taken the time to understand the target and their environment.

Conclusion

This is just a short chapter on the basics of gathering human intelligence but can also be used as a guide for counterintelligence if you just place yourselves in the target's place.

Where budgets are available there are plenty of electronic surveillance options available these days but if you do not have the budget then the low-tech traditional methods of gathering human intelligence are still as reliable today as they were thousands of years ago when people started spying on each other,

which I expect was about the same time they learned how to walk
and talk...

COUNTER-SURVEILLANCE

If you are engaged in investigating corrupt officials, criminals or terrorists you must understand the basics of counter-surveillance. Be assured, if these people find out you are looking into their businesses and activities, they will target you.

If you are serious about your personal security, basic counter-surveillance procedures should be part of your daily routine. The reason you need to understand counter-surveillance is to identify anyone who has you under surveillance. Take precautions when you leave and enter your home or office and especially when you're meeting with informants or sources.

In nearly all burglaries, muggings, robberies, assassinations, or kidnappings the criminals or terrorists will put their target under surveillance to assess their target's routines and the level of personal security. If you're operating in an area where professional organized criminal groups or narco-terrorists are active you can be assured, they will be employing multi-layered surveillance programs to identify threats to their organizations and to identify potential targets for kidnapping or extortion.

Counter-surveillance is the base skill for all personal security programs. In this short chapter, I am going to highlight some of the main considerations for a counter-surveillance plan and detail some simple but effective street drills that will enable you to identify if you are under surveillance.

Many supposed security professionals put a lot of time, effort and money into firearms and unarmed combat training, but very few spend any time or effort on their surveillance and counter-surveillance skills.

Professional surveillance operatives put their targets into three categories: unaware, aware and professional. Most people, I would say at least 75%, fall into the unaware category: you can follow them around all day, and they won't realize you're there. Give it a try the next time you're out at the mall! About 24% of people would fall into the aware category and would realize, after a while if someone was watching or following them. The 1% left would fall into the professional category; they take active counter-surveillance measures and would spot people acting suspicious, watching or following them. So, I expect most people reading this chapter are in the unaware category but by the time you finish reading this, there is no reason not to be in the professional category.

The Basics

You can start training while you're reading this chapter. Look around where you are now, if you're in an office look out the window. Are there any people hanging around on the street or sitting in parked cars for no apparent reason? If they are still there in 30 minutes and there is no logical reason, what are they up to, what's their body language saying, are they being over observant? People don't hang around the streets and sit in parked cars for no reason unless they are on surveillance or up to something!

Learning to read people's body language is an extremely important skill. If someone is on surveillance or looking to commit a crime, the chances are they will be acting differently than those around them. Most people do not pay attention to their surroundings, so if someone is over observant, what are they up to?

When you are out at the mall or in a restaurant or bar, watch the people around you and try to identify what mood they are in or what type of discussion they are having with others. It should be easy to identify if a man and a woman are on a romantic date or two business people are having a heated discussion. When in a coffee shop try to determine what people are looking at on their laptops; are they concentrating or goofing around. Learning to read body language is of paramount importance because it will help you identify, avoid and if necessary, react to potential threats.

A basic counter-surveillance plan for your home, business or office would be to simply look around the general area and identify the location(s) from which you could be watched, then check it from time to time. If someone is hanging around that area take note; if they are there for an extended time or show up regularly, what are they doing?

These days if you're drawing up a counter-surveillance plan you need to take surveillance cameras into consideration. There is a vast array of affordable surveillance cameras on the market that can be used either defensively, to watch potential surveillance locations you've identified, or offensively, by someone intent to spy on you. For example, at a very basic level, why sit outside someone's house and watch them when you can place a $100 hunting trail camera in their garden? Retrieve it after a few days and you will have photos/video of all their comings and goings. If your budget allows it, why not place a camera connected to a GSM network that will send real-time images to your cell phone or email? Here I am talking about regular commercial hunting cameras available at Wal-Mart, not specialized remote surveillance cameras. But no worries, as I am sure everyone reading this regularly sweeps their gardens and parking lots for surveillance cameras, right?

I am old school and believe that you need to be able to operate with minimum equipment and support but should employ technology when you have access to it, just don't be 100% reliant on it. Nowadays drones are easily available to the public and can be used for surveillance and counter-surveillance. Things that need to be considered when using drones are their camera quality, flight time, weather conditions they will be used in and from the good guy's point of view, what are the laws regarding their use in your area. Even within a small-scale private security operation drones could be employed for estate security, for clearance, perimeter patrols, and route checks, etc.

To dominate the area around a location you would need to patrol it and pay special attention to potential surveillance locations, think like the criminals or terrorists and put yourself in their shoes: how would YOU watch YOURSELF? When I say patrol an area, I do not mean you need to dress up in tactical gear and pretend to be Robo-Cop. You can patrol an area by going for a casual walk, walking a dog or taking a bicycle ride, etc. While patrolling you want to look for people or cars that are out of place, cameras, and ground signs that people have been waiting in specific locations such as cigarette butts, trash, or trampled vegetation.

Overt patrols only draw attention and will alert your opposition that you are taking active measures, which will then up their skill level and cause them to retreat to farther out positions. If you identify you are under surveillance without alerting your opposition, there are many ways to exploit the situation. How you do so will depend on the overall circumstances of the operation, your resources, and the laws you are working under. All of this needs to be considered in your operational planning.

In urban areas surveillance operatives use as cover locations where people congregate, such as cafés, bars, bus stops or payphones. If someone is sitting in the coffee shop across the road from your office all day they may just be working there, but if you see them on the subway or at another location, then maybe you have a stalker, private investigator, or criminal on your tail.

If you think you are under surveillance you need to establish why and who the threat is: criminals, government, a lone stalker, private investigators, or a crazy ex. You need to do this, so you can determine their potential skill level and consider what other type of surveillance is being used against you: listening devices, remote cameras, mail being intercepted, computers being hacked or physical surveillance?

These days we must ensure our computers, smartphones and internet connections are secure; if the criminals or terrorists get access to these, for most people it means they will know all their personal details. I am still surprised that currently a lot of people still have no security on their phones or computers, post personal information, and photos on public social media accounts. I think these days it's suspicious if someone does not use social media to some extent, personally I think most platforms are safe enough, just understand whatever you post is or can become public.

Computer and network security are a constantly evolving specialized industry that needs to be left to the experts, but social engineering is something everyone in the security industry needs to understand. In basic terms, social engineering is some form of confidence trick used to gather intelligence, defraud or get access to computer systems, etc. A lot of successful computer hacks are just successful social engineering operations rather than network penetrations. Social engineering operations are disguised as regular everyday happenings that fit in with the target's lifestyle. For example, the bored middle-aged CEO gets a Facebook friend request from an attractive young lady, he confirms the request and starts chatting and trying to impress her. The young lady's Facebook profile can be a complete fraud made up by those targeting the CEO or other members of his corporation. By just confirming the friend request the CEO has given the criminals or terrorists access to a wealth of information, and will give up more in his ongoing conversations and hopefully emails from his corporate account...

Just think about how many people can access your computer, for example colleagues at your office. If you leave your computer at the office overnight can maintenance, security or cleaning staff get access to it? There have been cases of corporate espionage where private detective agencies have placed agents in the cleaning and security staff working at their target's offices, so they can access the target company's computers and trash after work hours. Most people would not consider as a threat the bumbling night shift security guard or the apparently barely literate office cleaner. Both could be downloading business data from the company's computers or copying confidential papers, and they should be viewed as a threat!

You cannot carry your computers around with you all the time so, one thing to do is to keep minimum information on it. Keep all your sensitive information on a thumb drive or hard drive, which you can always keep on your person. Then if someone accesses your computer or if it's lost or stolen the criminals won't get any worthwhile information.

The next time you are in a coffee shop for example, without being obvious, look at what people are doing on their computers, phones and listen in to their conversations. Many people regularly work in public locations where anyone can view their computer screens, with unsecured Wi-Fi connections with the same comfort level they would have at home. When chatting with friends in public, people disclose all the time personal information that could be useful to a criminal. So, remember, if you can view what others are doing on their computers or phones and listen to their conversations, others could do the same to you if given the opportunity.

If you believe your computers or phones are bugged then you need to get them cleaned, which can be costly and difficult in some locations. Another option is to use misinformation to mislead or entrap those who may be monitoring you. This could be a safer option rather than letting the criminals or terrorists know that their operation is compromised, which could force them into acting.

Street Drills

You must always be on the lookout for criminal surveillance and here I have listed a few simple drills, which are used by professional criminals and intelligence operatives alike. These simple drills will help you identify anyone who is watching or following you. First, let me give you an example from the mid-1990s when I was part of a commercial surveillance team in central London whose task was to watch a target that turned out to be in the professional category.

The people running the job had placed a surveillance vehicle, an old British Telecom van, across the road from the target's hotel. The target, I expect, identified the van quickly; tinted rear windows, parked in one position for an extended period, etc. If I remember correctly on the first day the target left the hotel, jumped into a black cab and we lost him straight away due to traffic. On day two the target took the subway and went for a walk around the West End of London. He used several of the counter-surveillance drills I have listed here and ripped the surveillance team apart! Those running the job resorted to placing a pseudo-married couple in the hotel to try to observe what the target was doing and talking about in the bar and restaurant. Running surveillance on aware and professional targets can be extremely difficult, it's not like the movies. You should always be at the aware level but preferably professional level of awareness and it's not difficult to accomplish that!

Adapt a few of these drills to your situation, they are simple and proven.

• When walking on the street, turn around and walk back the same way you came; remember the people you walk past or anyone that stops. Also, remember to check on the opposite side of the street for anyone stopping, etc. Do this several times and if you see the same person or couples more than once, they may be following you.

• If you are driving, do a couple of U-turns, watch for anyone doing the same and the cars you pass. If you see the same car a couple of times you may be being followed.

• Walk around a corner, stop, and remember the first few people that come after you. Again, do this several times and, if you see the same person more than once, they may be following you. Watch the body language of those that come around the corner after you, any flinch could be an indication you have surprised them. You can also do the same when you're driving. From a personal security standpoint remember to always take corners wide as you never know what's waiting for you on the other side.

• Escalators are good for counter-surveillance because while ascending, you can have a good look around at who is behind you. A simple drill would be to go up an escalator and straight back down again. If anyone is following you, they would have to do the same.

• Take special note of people waiting in parked cars, especially near your residence or office. Be especially suspicious of any unattended vans with blacked-out windows parked close to your residence or office. Vans are the most common surveillance and snatch vehicles. As the saying goes: there are only two reasons for two people to be waiting in a car for no apparent reason: they are either having sex or they are on surveillance.

• Do not board trains or buses until the last minute; anyone boarding after you should be treated as suspect.

• Jump on a bus, tram or metro and jump off one stop later and see if anyone else does the same. People usually don't bother getting on a bus to go only 200 yards.

• Go into a café and covertly watch what goes on in the street. Look out for people waiting around to follow you when you leave or anyone who keeps walking past the café, they could be trying to see what you're doing. Pay special attention to locations where people are congregating for legitimate reasons, such as bus stops, cafés, etc...

• Walk across open spaces such as parks or squares and see if anyone is running around the outside of the open area trying to keep up with you- they must do this because there is no cover for them in the open space and the distance to go around the open space is greater than walking straight across it.

• Use reflections from windows and other surfaces to see who is behind you or use the selfie camera on your cell phone.

• Watch out for people who look out of place or are waiting in the same spot for a long time, such as waiting at a bus stop without getting on any buses or at a payphone for an extended period.

• Be aware of people waiting in a location by themselves, especially fit, young men with short hair. Chances are they are criminals or police. Professional surveillance teams usually consist of mixed couples in their 30's to 50's. Criminals regularly use children, so be wary!

• If you think someone is following you, do not acknowledge them, just slow down and stop to look in shop windows, or go into a café and have a coffee. If you still see the person waiting around, you are most probably under surveillance.

• When you're driving, drive slowly, and take note of anyone doing the same, occasionally pull over and make note of the cars that go past you, if you see the same car more than once you might have a problem.

• If you do not want to look directly at someone who could be following you, look at their feet and remember their shoes. Very few people wear the same shoes, check this out the next time you are out. If you keep seeing the same pair of shoes at various locations, this person could be following you.

• Criminals following you may change their hair, jackets and pants, etc. to try and disguise themselves but they rarely change their shoes. The same goes for jewelry or watches, it can be difficult to give a description of someone so look for distinctive jewelry, tattoos, type of cell phone or anything that makes them stand out. If the person is completely nondescript, chances are they are pros.

• If you think someone is following you check their dress to see if they could be concealing cameras or weapons. Are they always on their cell phone possibly describing your actions or taking photos? What does their body language say, do they look nervous, over observant, or as if they are concentrating too much, etc.?

• Be suspicious of unknown people who start conversations with you- they could be testing your reactions and personal security level.

• You need to be extra vigilant when attending any meetings. In high-risk situations, these could have been set up by the opposition to photograph you or set you up to be kidnapped or assassinated. Always sweep the area for anything suspicious - people or vehicles - before attending the meeting.

• If you think the opposition is trying to get photos or video of you, meet in places where there is low light, like dark restaurants and stay in the shadows as most cameras will not be able to get decent pictures.

• If you believe someone is trying to get audio recordings of you, meet in a crowded place and keep your voice low. The noise from other people or traffic, etc. would be picked up by any microphones and can cover your conversation.

• To check whether the person with whom you are meeting is under surveillance, turn up 5 minutes late and sweep the area for anyone suspicious. Try to take the person you're meeting with to another location and do a couple of discreet counter-surveillance maneuvers along the way.

• Stop regularly to make telephone calls or look in shop windows as this will allow you to observe your surroundings and identify anyone who may be following you.

• Use underground trains whenever available- radios and mobile phones usually don't work underground. This will cause problems for any surveillance team as they won't be able to communicate with each other.

• You must make plans on what procedures you will carry out if you are under surveillance. These will depend on where you are and the threat you are under. These days if you think you're being watched, chances are the criminals, terrorists or stalker have already tried to hack your phone or computer, so get them cleaned up and secured!

From a personal security point of view if you are on the street and you seriously think you are being followed get to a safe area as soon as possible and call for someone trusted to come and pick you up. From a close protection operations point of view, there are various tactics you can employ if you want to identify those following you or to warn them off, all depends on where you are and the overall operational plan.

In First World countries, you can inform the police, but I strongly expect they won't take the call seriously unless there is a domestic restraining order in place or there is a case history. If you or your client are being stalked you need to start building up evidence against the stalker, take videos and keep a log of the occurrences. If someone is watching your home or business call the police and report it, if they are not busy, they may respond and question the individual, etc. Depending on the case this could lead to a loitering ticket, an arrest or nothing, but a least you have a record of calling the police for your file.

I've had numerous clients over the years who've had issues with private detectives following and watching them. If you are being stalked and harassed by private detectives call the police on them, they have no special authority, their badges just mean they are licensed, if that. They cannot trespass, go through garbage, or inhibit your lifestyle, etc. If the police can't help, then a written complaint to their licensing authority with evidence of their actions tends to work!

This is a short chapter on a very important and in-depth subject that cannot be learned from a book, I hope it makes you think about your personal security procedures and assists you in your operational planning.

COVERT COMMUNICATIONS GUIDE

The basis for good communications security these days is understanding that all electronic communications and devices are not secure. All hardware such as phones and computers as well as software and applications are hackable or have a backdoor that are provided to governments as part of the licensing agreements. Remember no communications are 100% secure from eavesdropping or interception.

In many countries corrupt government officials and employees of intelligence agencies work hand in hand with criminal groups and sell intercepted communications or will work directly for the criminals. Also, many employees of phone and internet companies have access to the users of their networks data, locations, phone call and messaging records, all of which can be given to government agencies or sold to those with sufficient cash. All communications that go through mobile phone towers and communication companies' servers leaves a history.

Also, there is the threat from devices that can intercept mobile communications such as IMSI-Catchers. An international mobile subscriber identity-catcher, or IMSI-catcher, is a mobile eavesdropping device used for intercepting mobile phone traffic and tracking location data of mobile phone users. The IMSI-catchers are essentially a "fake" mobile communications tower that acts in between the target mobile phone and the service provider's real towers, it is considered a man-in-the-middle attack.

IMSI-Catchers are restricted items that require government documentation to buy, just the same as weapons systems. But they are available for purchase on the black market from corrupt government officials or manufacturers that are based in locations or sell in or through locations that have weak communications laws and restrictions. For example, IMSI catchers are used in many African countries, in one country it was reported that the foreign operators of the IMSI-catchers were selling the retrieved data and communications to both sides involved in a contested and heated election.

All smartphone applications have backdoors and are monitored. Such applications as WhatsApp etc. would not be given operating licenses if they did not cooperate with the authorities in the countries where their apps are used. In numerous countries messaging apps and voice calling apps are blocked for national security issues.

There have also been some messaging applications that have been set up by government agencies specifically for catching and intercepting criminals', journalists, and activists communications. The ANOM messaging app was jointly invented by the Australian Police and the US FBI. Smartphones and computers with the ANOM app installed on them were distributed to known criminals, allowing police to monitor their chats about drug smuggling, money laundering and even murder plots. Another example is the EncroChat encrypted messaging app that was penetrated by French intelligence agencies and led to the arrest of over 700 suspected criminals in the UK and Europe.

Also, some supposedly private encrypted email servers have given over their users' data to law enforcement agencies. In 2021 the encrypted-email company ProtonMail publicly admitted it handed over the details of its users to authorities even though this Swiss company sells itself on its complete privacy of their users' personal data. Protonmail said it had been legally obliged to collect data from an account said to be linked to a "climate activist" who was arrested by French police.

Spyware is also a major threat and can easily be installed and downloaded onto a target's device. If you lose control of your phone or computer for even a limited time and if falls into the hands of those seeking to target you, spyware can be installed which will turn your personal device into an enemy controlled device that will be spying on you 24/7.

Spyware can also be installed by opening unknown links and downloading unknown applications from 3rd party servers. So, you must keep your communication devices physically secure, do not talk with strangers online or open any unknown links or attachments. A well published spyware infection was that of the Israeli made Pegasus spyware that was used by governments to spy on activists, journalists, political opponents, and even foreign government official, one of whom was reported to be the former British prime minister "Liz Truss"!

So, these days it's essential for Investigative Journalists, political activists, or private investigators to be very careful how they communicate and store data and content, especially in potentially hostile environments and situations. What I will do here is give you some guidance on how by using simple techniques you can minimize the risk of your electronic communications being compromised.

• Always try to keep the devices you use for work and personal use separate. If you are working on a specific case or story that requires secure communications buy a device specifically for that job and use it only for communications to do with that job. By doing this if you are ever at risk of being compromised or arrested you can always destroy that phone or reset to factory settings to wipe clean its memory.

• Consider if the source of your phone could have been compromised? Did you buy the device randomly or was it pre-ordered or pre-owned? Could those that gave or sold you the device had placed spyware on it knowing you would be using it? Likewise, if you are using a sim, was its source possibly compromised? It's better to buy devices, sims and memory cards etc. from random dealers. Be very suspicious of people who want to give you phones or computers, if you accept at lease reset them to the factory settings to try to delete any hidden spyware but I would not use them for sensitive cases.

• Always use a decent VPN service and regularly scan the phone or computer for any unusual applications or programs.

• Most smartphones will operate with Wi-Fi without a sim card, you do not need a phone number or data and can use the phone on Wi-Fi for communications via selected apps or via email. Always ensure that the Bluetooth is turned off and the phone is set to airplane mode.

• You need to select various Wi-Fi locations such as cafes or businesses where you can log on to the internet for free. Vary these locations as much as possible, never use the same location on the same days at the same times etc.

• When using a café or restaurants Wi-Fi always ensure that you are a good customer, buy drinks and food etc. that way they will be happy for you to sit there and be online. Have a cover story prepared if they ask why, you are there for a long time. Taking a friend with you can help you to blend in better, as two friends talking for a few hours is normal, whereas a lone man drinking one cup of coffee for a few hours can be suspicious!

• When you have access to the internet you can download applications that don't need phone numbers to operate. For example, fake Instagram and Facebook accounts can be set up with just an email address and have good messenger services.

• There is a wide array of free email service where temporary email accounts can be set up for specific jobs and contacts. To login to most email services, you only need access to a web browser like Google or better still Firefox.

• Once you have set up your accounts memorize the usernames and passwords and always log out of the accounts. This way you can always access these accounts wherever you are on any device.

• Try to also remember the social media handles and online names of contacts you may need to contact in case of emergency or if you lose or need to throw away your device.

• In high-risk situations you can download and install the applications you are using for communications or photo and data storage onto your device each time you need to use them. When the messages have been sent or photos or data uploaded then the application can be deleted. Your messages would have been sent and your photos etc. stored until the next time you download and login to the applications. Ensure the devices history is always cleaned out as that way if your phone is searched by anyone targeting you it will be clean.

• Setting up email accounts or cloud storage etc. and sharing the login details with the people you are talking to or working with is another way of communicating. That way no messages or data is being sent and information and photos can be uploaded and downloaded as required in draft messages etc.

• Micro-SD memory cards are excellent for data and photo storage and most smartphones use them for extra internal storage. They are small, easy to hide and can, depending on the model hold a lot of data. A basic 32GB card can hold thousands of photos, documents and hours of video. When traveling all sensitive data can be removed from your devices and placed on a micro-SD card and concealed in the lining of a jacket, inside a shoe or among other regular items.

• Where available pay phones, mobile phones that are being rented for calls or call shops can be used for voice calls. But remember call shops can record conversations and will be storing all phone numbers called. Vary the use of pay phones and public calling services as much as possible, do not set any patterns in your activities.

• Today, it is generally assumed that telephone communications are not secure. It is usually safe, however, when previous arrangements have been made, for two people to go to different public telephone booths at the same time and then carry on their conversation without the use of any suspicious words or phrases. Simple codes can be used.

• Internet cafés and business suites can be used for online communications but remember that the computers can be monitored and remember to always clear the history and cookies of any public computer you use. If you do not clear the history and cookies others can see the sites, you visited and even possibly your passwords and login details. Be careful and understand how to wipe the history and cookies on any public computers you use or even borrow from friends.

An example of how, what I have written about here could be applied could go like the following: An investigative journalist is going to a country to interview a source for a serious story on human rights violations and corruption. He flies to the country with his personal phone that has nothing to do with the story or his contacts within that country on it.

When he arrives in the country, after ensuring he is not being followed, he goes to a random phone shop and buys a smartphone. He then proceeds to a café where he logs onto their free internet and with his new phone logs into the email service that he has previously set up to communicate with his contacts. A meeting is arranged.

At the meeting his contacts give him a micro-SD card containing documents and photos to do with the story. The following day the journalist goes to another café, downloads a cloud storage application onto his new phone and uploads the documents and photos from the micro-SD card that he has placed in his new phone. When the upload is complete, he uninstalls the cloud storage application from the phone. He has the option now to destroy the micro-SD card or to conceal it to take with him when he leaves the country.

If the journalist needs to interview anyone then the interviews could be recorded onto his new phone, uploaded, from a different café to the cloud application or an email account, or stored on the micro SD card.

As this is a high-risk situation the journalist has a trusted associate outside of the country downloading everything that he is uploading in case the journalist is arrested, or the online accounts are compromised. When the trusted contact signals that they have downloaded and stored all the uploaded documents and photos the journalist destroys the micro-SD card.

As the journalist leaves the country, he resets the phone he bought to factory settings, takes it apart and throws it in various garbage cans. All evidence of his activities has now been erased. He will leave the country with his personal phone which will just have tourist photos etc. on it. If searched there is nothing that could compromise the journalist or his contacts. Remember traveling with a phone that has been wiped clean and is set on the factory settings is suspicious for police or airport authorities.

As another example, this time from a real task I undertook for a client who was having problems in let's say an emerging market. The client was caught up in a legal dispute over several maritime vessels which had been seized by the authorities of the country they were in. The client needed to confirm the vessels were in good order and not being dismantled. They had just given a large amount of money to a very high-profile investigation agency to go and do this task for them but were not happy with the results.

This investigations company had sent two of its specialist operatives to the country to check things out; they took with them the latest encrypted satellite phone for secure communications which initially impressed the client when they showed it to them and gave them a story of how they planned to complete the operation.

The country they were going to had very suspicious and alert government security agencies. Even though the country is supposedly poor as far as the media portrays it, the city they were traveling to was very modern. However, if these wannabe James Bonds had been stopped at customs, the expensive encrypted satellite phone would immediately draw attention to them... Why does someone need an encrypted satellite phone in a modern city?

The client was contacted by the operatives when they were in the country, but they contacted him by a regular landline phone, because they could not get a signal on the encrypted satellite phone. Satellite phones operate on specific networks that are monitored and can be blocked in some locations as was the case here.

The operatives told the client they could not locate the vessels and asked the client where he thought they might be. He did not know and asked them if they had asked the harbor master in the city's port. They had not, because neither of them could speak the local language.

In the end, they located someone to speak to the harbor master and found the vessels. The operators then drew up plans which detailed how they could steal one of the vessels, which would have been highly illegal. This was when the client's patience had run out and they contacted me.

Within our network, we had a local contact within the country and had them monitor the vessels. All communications were done using encrypted e-mail; almost everyone has computers and smartphones these days and, as long as you have an internet access, you can send messages globally in just few seconds.

E-mails are monitored and can be easily intercepted, which is why they should be encrypted. Good encryption software can be downloaded from the Internet for free or used via secure internet providers such as Tutamail, so there is no excuse not to use this technology. There are millions of e-mails being sent every day, many more than encrypted satellite phone messages. Basic rule: always blend in with your environment!

One of the more simple but sophisticated ways of using online communication to avoid detection is the use of virtual dead drops in the form of anonymous sharing portals. Anonymous sharing portals such as, https://telegra.ph/ & https://justpaste.it/ have no-login requirement and provide anonymity. When the messages are written on the portal their links can be shared and distributed.

The following techniques are used by intelligence agencies worldwide, they are simple, effective, low-tech and work in environments where electronic communications are completely compromised or when you need to move large amounts of documents, photos or video evidence. Low-tech non-electronic communications techniques can be divided into two types:

• **Personal communications:** Personal communications include face-to-face discussions, either between two participating parties or with the active assistance of intermediaries.

• **Non-personal communications:** Non-personal communications may involve mail, notices placed in newspapers, magazines or social media sites, messages left in hiding places to be picked up later by another person, etc.

Both personal and non-personal forms of communication have both advantages and disadvantages.

Face-to-face meetings are extremely dangerous in times of an active threat or when sensitive information is being handled. Therefore, they should be well planned in advance, so that the maximum amount of benefit can be guaranteed from a meeting of the shortest possible duration. If subsequent meetings are required, they should be varied as to the location, time of day or the day of the week.

In selecting a time and place for personal meetings, the general character of the area must be taken into consideration. The location will depend heavily on the threat level and what the opposition is trying to uncover. You will need a logical reason for being in that area at the time scheduled. In the event that either party decides they may have been followed, they should have some legitimate activity which they can take care of and then leave again without it compromising the person they were planning to meet. Both parties must have a plausible and convincing cover story which will explain their activities at that time and place. Alternate times and places for the meeting should have been decided on in advance, in case one or both parties are not able to make the first scheduled meeting.

Both parties involved will also need a covert way of alerting the other person that they are under surveillance. Additionally, along the route that each will travel to the meeting place, certain signal posts should have been selected in advance. These are areas in which a sign of some kind could be left by either party who wished to warn off the other so that they would not approach the meeting spot and fall into a possible trap. A chalk mark on a specific wall or crushed chalk of a specific color or a piece of fruit on a pavement can be used to represent a multitude of signals and messages.

Phones are not recommended ways of warning people off when you are under surveillance, phone calls and messages leave a paper trail. The specific way your car is parked in a certain car park space can be used as a warning sign. Or you are reading a certain newspaper or magazine at the meeting spot could be a sign to the other person with whom you are meeting with to abort the meeting. Just as you drinking orange juice instead of coffee could send the message that things are safe for the meeting, use your imagination and keep it simple.

When you are meeting people for the first time, prearranged signs and counter signs should be used to confirm the identity of each person. Generally, the best coded sign is a question, and the best counter sign is an answer to that question. Both must contain predetermined words or phrases and each should be both short and simple in content and pronunciation. A simple example would be, question: Is it raining in Mombasa? Reply: No, it is very dusty! You need to always make sure those you are meeting with are the real people, so you don't end up in captivity or found strangled on a garbage dump!

The terms "cut out" and "live drop" are used frequently in intelligence networks and espionage organizations. A cut out is a person who carries messages back and forth between two other people that cannot meet personally without arousing suspicion. The cut out is often an active participant in the conversations and may make plans, us his own means of persuasion or participate in negotiations himself.

The term live drop applies to a person that merely accepts a message or item from one person and holds until another party can conveniently pick it up. The live drop must always be aware they are taking messages from legitimate sources; codes phrases should always be employed when accepting and passing on messengers as the couriers might vary and be unknown to the live drop.

For the sake of security, the amount of information given to cut outs is usually no more than is required for their task. At times a message left with a live drop may be given to them verbally, memorized and passed on verbally to the pickup. One good option is to encrypt or place in a password protected vault app any documents, photos etc. and put them on a micro-SD card or thumb drive that can be passed to a live drop for a pickup.

Non-personal communications generally provide greater safety for the participants, but they add an element of chance as far as the security and the accuracy of the transmission of the messages are concerned, and also the possibility of interception. The third party used for a cut-out or live drop must be 100% trustworthy and are personal security and counter surveillance aware.

The term "dead drop" refers to a hiding place where someone may leave a message to be picked up later by another person. The advantages and disadvantages in the use of dead drops are these: dead drop communications are safer as there is no direct contact between the sender and the recipient of the message. Dead drops are more secure, because the recipient does not need to know the identity of the person who leaves the message for them. Likewise, the person who leaves the message does not need to know the identity of the person who picks it up. Dead drops provide a greater flexibility of time in the event it is difficult for both the sender and receiver of the message to be in the same area on the same date.

One disadvantage in the use of dead drops is that the message is out of control for a certain length of time. It may be accidentally found, it may be destroyed or perhaps intercepted by the threat without participants' immediate knowledge. Dead drops may be stationary or mobile. One example of a stationary dead drop could be a hollow limb of a tree in some public park, or an apparently abandoned tin can or old bottle lying in the middle of a weed patch that can contain a message or micro-SD card etc.

Wide use can be made of magnetic key boxes / containers as they can be attached to anything iron or steel. For example, they can be placed on the bumper of a bus or truck as it leaves one terminal or gas station and can be taken off by a receiving operative in some other city as the bus comes into the terminal or the trucks stops to fill up its gas tanks.

In the use of dead drops, it is customary to leave a signal in some public spot or on a social media post to indicate that a message has been placed in the dead drop. In this way, it is not necessary for the intended recipient of the message to risk themselves unnecessarily by going repeatedly to a dead drop when no message may be waiting for them there. Always check the area around a dead drop location before approaching it to ensure it has not been compromised and is under surveillance or being ambushed by threat personnel.

When you have reason to travel legitimately to another area, you should always use this opportunity to scout out possible meeting places or possible locations where hidden messages might be left to be picked up later.

Codes should be used between group members. For example, a bodyguard may not live with his client but can call them several times a day, if the client mentions a certain word or phrase during the call, it could mean there is a problem etc.

Various objects of clothing hanging on a clothesline, certain lights left on in various rooms of a house at a certain time, a parked car left facing either north or south, a certain hat worn askew either to the left or to the right are all typical signals that may be used as a covert warning or to convey information. Use your imagination, there are endless things that can be used and simple but effective warning and messaging systems.

All of these things remind us once again that the requirements of security are in conflict with the requirements for speed and efficiency where communications are concerned. It is very easy to become so security minded that your efficiency is badly impaired. There will always be times when speed is of the essence and when security precautions must be thrown to the wind. In most cases, however, covert communications techniques should be used which will provide a reasonable balance between speed, efficiency, and security.

The conclusion of this chapter is that you must remember that no electronic communications or devices are secure, so you need to be extremely careful. By following the guidelines here, you will help to minimize the risk of being compromised by those actively targeting you.

ELECTRONIC SURVEILLANCE

Electronic surveillance is a main intelligence gathering resource for governments, criminals, terrorists and private investigators. You need to understand that you can employ electronic surveillance when you are targeting others but, it can also be used against you!

It is easy to get hold of listening devices (bugs), bugging equipment and covert cameras from commercial outlets and the many shops that specialize in making and supplying this type of equipment. Today, many bugs and covert cameras can be hidden in almost any objects like books, computers, mobile phones, rocks, and clothing. You should always take precautions against bugs and covert cameras, especially when you are staying in hotels or moving into a new residence.

There are thousands of devices on the commercial market that claim to be able to detect bugs. However, bugs work on many different frequencies or on GSM networks and many commercially available bugs and bug detectors work on only a small sector of frequencies available. A professional criminal or terrorist will always try to use bugs that are outside of the usual frequencies or on GSM networks, so they stand less chance of detection. In addition, you must take into consideration remote-controlled bugs that can be turned on and off by the listener. With most equipment, you would not pick up this type of bug, because it would usually be turned off until needed, such as during a meeting. In this sector, the most expensive equipment is not always the best. If you consider buying it, make sure it does what the maker claims.

If your threat is from electric surveillance (ES), you should employ the services of a trusted specialist in the electronic counter-surveillance (ECM) field. Always check the credentials of the person you employ for this task and make sure he is trustworthy, also check out that his ECM kit is of a professional standard. An ECM specialist should also have the equipment that is required to find bugs that are not within the usual frequency ranges. If you use the services of a commercial ECM specialist, they must never be left unsupervised. There have been many cases where de-buggers have been found to be working for the opposition and planting or ignoring devices.

You should also be aware of the threat from "hard-wire" devices. These do not transmit information via the airways and cannot be detected by scanners, etc. A listen through a wall device is a good example of this type of device. The device could be placed on the outside of a meeting/hotel room and will pick up all the conversations taking place in the room. The device could be attached directly to a recorder, so there are no transmissions. There are government agencies claiming to have a microfiber device that they can stretch for 3 kilometers and receive good quality audio and video footage.

It would be unrealistic for you to always carry around with you ECM equipment. The best defense you have against these devices is to perform a physical search whenever you will be staying for some time in a room or moving into a new residence. You should always carry with you such equipment as a flashlight and a Swiss Army knife or type of tool. These basic items are all you should need to adequately perform a basic room search. If you anticipate that you will have to do an in-depth search, always take a full search kit.

How A Bug Could Be Placed

Consider this scenario: a criminal is targeting an executive for kidnapping. He needs to get information on the executive's movements, routine, etc. A simple tactic would be to place a listening device in the reception area of the target's office. The criminal would need to buy a simple, small listening device which could be bought over the internet or from a spy shop. The criminal would then task an associate, preferably female, to enter the reception area and ask the receptionists for directions, etc. While talking to the receptionists the female could blow her nose and ask them to let her put her tissue in their trash can. Wrapped in the tissue would be the bug. Who would ever ask to check a tissue someone has just blown their nose in! All going well the bug would now be in place and would pick up everything the receptionists are saying. Think about it, receptionists handle a lot of sensitive information: they make appointments, book taxis and restaurants, etc. A small bug could transmit for about 20 to 75 meters depending on its quality and the environment it's used in. If someone could not covertly get close enough to listen to it, a receiver attached to a digital voice activated recorder could be placed close by, in a flower bed or up a drainpipe, etc. GSM bugs use SIM cards so they can be listened to globally from any location with a phone connection.

Considerations

• Why might your client be under electronic surveillance?

• Who is the threat? Criminal, government, commercial, personal?

• What is the expected level of skill and equipment of the opposition?

• What information about you does the opposition have?

Counter Procedures

• Change meeting rooms and places at short notice- this will cause problems for anyone who was planning to put you under electronic surveillance.

• Search rooms prior to meetings.

• Clear everyone from the room/area before the search and then secure the area and allow access to authorized personnel only after the search is finished.

• Upgrade the security of all areas and employ your own personnel in a counter-surveillance role.

• Physically search the area for suspect vehicles which could be used as a receiving/relay point for transmissions from a bug.

• Leave enough time to search the area before the meeting starts.

• Meeting rooms should have minimal furniture as this gives the opposition fewer places to plant bugs.

• Search everyone entering meeting rooms for recorders or transmitters and make sure all rubbish is searched and removed.

• Check any vacant-adjoining buildings and physically search the outside of buildings.

• Perform counter-surveillance physical and electronic during meetings.

• Keep a frequency scanner on permanent scan.

• Be aware of remote-controlled bugs.

• Search pictures, sockets, phones, plugs, any gifts. Place tape over screw heads, check any new furnishings, check ceiling panels, check outside the room.

• Draw curtains or close blinds before those attending the meeting enter the room.

Cell/mobile phones can also be used as listening devices when set to auto-answer. Once they are put in place the threat just calls the phone to hear what is being said in the close vicinity around the phone. The only limitations cell phones have, are their size and battery life. The other issue with cell/mobile phones is that they can be hacked or have surveillance apps installed. There are many commercially available surveillance apps for cell/mobile phone monitoring. In high-crime areas where the criminals are working with the police and cell phone companies, they can monitor your calls and e-mails via the servers.

Another cover for planting electronic surveillance devices are burglaries. If you came home and found that your house or car had been broken into, would you be more worried about what had been stolen or what had been put in place? If your car, house or hotel room has been broken into they need to be searched for electronic surveillance devices and contraband. I mentioned cars here because they are favored areas to plant listening devices as they are generally easier for the criminal or private investigator to get access to and break into than a residence. Also, consider what you discuss in your car; many an extramarital affair has been discovered or confirmed by a voice-activated Dictaphone placed in a straying spouse's car.

Dictaphones on their own can be used by criminals as listening devices. When combined with a miniature microphone (that can be bought from most electronics stores) they make an excellent hardwire device. Dictaphones these days can record more than seventy-two hours and the data transfers easily to a computer. Consider how easy it would be for a criminal to get access to the outside walls or roof of the location you're in right now!!! Drill a small hole through to the inside and then place the microphone in the hole. Outside, the microphone wire could be camouflaged and the Dictaphone waterproofed and concealed, even buried. Then, every few days, the criminal could come by and swap the Dictaphone for one with fresh batteries and memory. The only way to find such a device would be a physical search; the $25K bug locator and the $500 an hour specialist would be nothing more than a waste of time and money.

Hopefully, after reading this chapter, you are more aware of the threat from electronic surveillance and how easy it is for even low-level criminals to use this means of gathering intelligence on an intended target.

BUGGING CONSIDERATIONS

The below notes were given to me years ago by someone who had worked for government agencies in the 1970's and 1980's. It's a list of considerations for planting electronic surveillance devices. Before everything went digital, staged burglaries were used as a cover for planting electronic listening devices and gathering non-admissible evidence. So, if a location has been burglarized or a car broken into, think about what could have been put in place, not just what's stolen.

- What information is needed?
- Where can we get it?
- Who from?
- Is there any other means of obtaining the information without bugging?
- If a bug is to be placed, then where, HOME, WORK, or VEHICLE?
- What are the consequences of the bug being found?
- Is the equipment to be left in place, if so, for how long? Does it need to be removed, if so what extra risks does this incur. If left in place what is the likelihood of it being discovered and what will be the consequences.
- Is there a safe place to monitor equipment from without leaving vehicles on the road?
- Does the target take any physical or electronic counter measures?
- Can results be gained by OVERT methods? For example, A. If the target is a businessman, can we make a legitimate appointment to meet him and bug the place whilst we are in the building? B. Can we gain access to the building by pos-

ing as a sales rep, telephone engineer, maintenance man or another type of tradesman? If so, you may need some type of disguise and a cover story including false I.D. and a checkable telephone number. C. Can we break into the office or home and use this 'break in' as a cover for planting an electronic device?

- To achieve this, we may need to force a door, a window or a skylight. We will actually need to steal something to cover our tracks; this now leaves us open to the criminal charge of burglary if caught. We may need to carry a jemmy, glass-cutter, bolt cutters or a cordless drill. We are now 'going equipped', which could be embarrassing if stopped by the police for a routine matter. We need to work out immediate action drills in case we are disturbed during the breaking and entering (B&E). Consider your actions if caught by 1. the police, 2. a member of the public, 3. the target. Do you, offer resistance, run, or give yourself up. Have you got a cover story ready for each eventuality?

- Let us now consider making a COVERT entry into the target area. We may need to consider some of the following points.

1. We may need to mount a full-scale physical surveillance operation against the target and or his premises. We will need to note the movements, timings and general routines of the target himself and possibly his family, employees, friends, visiting tradesmen and immediate neighbors. Are the target premises in a good position to carry out this type of in-depth surveillance? Does time permit? Has the target or his immediate neighbors got a dog, CCTV, or other security devices such as proximity lights, which will hamper you at night?

2. Have you got the knowledge and practical expertise to B&E without leaving evidence of your visit? If not do

you have the necessary contacts to get someone? Will they have the necessary knowledge to plant electronic bugging equipment effectively, or will they have to be escorted thus increasing the risks of being spotted? Do you want them to know what you are up to? Can you trust them, especially if it came to police interrogation? If you do have the capability to B&E yourself you will need, lock picking equipment or a lock pick gun, and gloves etc. You will need to use untraceable bugging equipment. You will also need to destroy all forensic evidence linking you to the scene, such as clothes, footwear etc. You should also have a reliable alibi prepared.

3. You should post lookouts with radios on a secure net using coded signals to provide early warning. These may also be able to act as a diversion to delay the police or any curios neighbors, or even the target returning unexpectedly. In Some circumstances it may be tactically possible to keep the target either occupied during the operation or under surveillance throughout to ensure that he does not return unexpectedly.

4. Once entry to the premises has been gained you should consider the following points: 1. Are any silent alarms or CCTV in operation? 2. Can you be seen from outside? 3. Have you locked the door behind you? 4. Can you photograph documents while you are there, do you need to use flash photography? 5. Use of a Polaroid camera can help to ensure that when you are searching drawers or moving things about, you replace them in the right places. 6. What type of bugs are you going to use, how long will they operate for effectively, remembering that your transmission range will decrease as the batteries run down. Mains powered bugs are usually the best for long term surveillance so consider placing wall socket bugs

in as many rooms as possible. Likewise, a teleinfinity device on the telephone can be accessed from anywhere in the world. You may even consider using a remote video smoke detector camera. If the target takes electronic countermeasures all bugs planted will have to be remotely operated so that they can be switched off during electronic sweeps. These types of bugs are usually only vulnerable to physical searches.

- This type of operation can be fairly risky or because of security measures difficult to mount. Therefore, consider the following alternative methods, A. Can you gain access to the telephone line from outside? B. Can you place a spike mic or wall contact mic anywhere on an outside wall or window? Also, if full electronic surveillance coverage of the target is required remember to bug the grounds or gardens outside. Ensure that all equipment used outside is weather proofed. C. Can you gain access via a garage or shed etc. to an inner wall, or the roof? D. Can a seed mic be used anywhere for example in cracks in the walls, under doors, floors, window frames or gaps in slates around the roof area. E. Is it possible to hire, rent or gain access to the adjoining property to the target premises?

- Even access to the building opposite may offer surveillance possibilities using parabolic or laser mics. If an adjacent room to the target room can be accessed it should be possible to use wall contact mics, fiber optic equipment allowing audio and visual surveillance or possibly seed mics. One method to achieve this would be to gain legitimate access to the target room on the pretext of a meeting, general enquiry etc. Whilst in the target room being interviewed or whatever, we recce the room. We are looking for wall fittings, paintings, pictures, calendars or wall charts etc. We note the exact location of any that are present. At a later date we can drill a small hole very carefully from the adjoining property, through the wall, behind a picture or chart and insert a fiber optic device or seed mic.

- One final point with making a COVERT entry. Under UK law if you B&E without causing any damage and you do not steal anything, then you are only guilty of trespass and not burglary.

PHOTOGRAPHY

It always amazes me how many people in the investigation, close protection and even media world can't take decent photographs or videos. Most cell phones come with cameras that can take decent stills photos and video that is more than adequate for operational purposes, so there is no excuse why people can't take photos these days.

I regularly come across private investigators and people who have completed close protection and firearms courses but have no clue how to take a half decent photo or video. If you ask me what is more relevant, knowing how to use a firearm or knowing how to use a camera, I will say knowing how to use a camera is priority. Knowing how to use firearms maybe a required skill, but it's not a priority for most people and if taught properly, it does not take long to get someone up to an OK operational standard.

These days photography is simple compared to what it used to be say 20 years ago. Back in the day you had to understand such things as shutter speeds, exposures and film speed, these days you can just point and shoot. I still have my old stills camera, a manual SLR with a 300mm lens, with a x2 converter to boost it up to 600mm, a 28mm wide angle lens and filters. These days most cell phone cameras are way more effective, versatile and powerful than my old SLR and its accessories.

The issue with professional SLR cameras for private investigators and close protection work is their size, walking around with an SLR camera and a large lens draws attention, especially if you're pointing it at someone. For static or mobile observation posts sure, they have an application, but for everyday street use, I would say their applications are limited. Even back in the day I tended to use zoom compact cameras a lot more than my SLR for no other reason than they were a lot more discreet.

Many times, I have heard expert private investigators telling their students and staff etc. to always buy the best equipment they can afford, don't go for the cheap option. This I can understand if you're in a government agency or spending money that's not yours, but I will always say buy what's adequate to get the job done. The issue with buying equipment that's going to be used for operations is that it's going to be banged around, abused and ultimately broken. Also, remember if you are looking to lend your cameras to those working for you they will not look after them, why should they, they didn't pay for them!

Why spend $2500 on a fancy camera when you can get a decent refurbished cell phone for $200 that can do the job just as well, more money in your pocket right! Of course, you will get better picture quality with a professional camera, but you must ask yourself how high of a definition do you need the photos to be? If you're looking to sell your photos and become a professional photographer a $5000 camera maybe a good investment. If you spend $5000 on a camera just hoping to get some surveillance work, then I will say you have been given some really bad advice!

Even if you're traveling you can buy smartphones with decent cameras at airports or on the streets virtually everywhere these days. So, if security is an issue, you can buy a smartphone at an airport, use it to take what photos you need, upload the photos or video via a Wi-Fi hotspot, delete the pics/apps, then dump or resell the phone before you leave the country, you don't even need a sim card. These days you must always remember to keep your online accounts, and your communication devices secure but that's another subject…

Photography, both stills and video, have a lot of applications in private investigations and close protection operations, a picture can speak 1000 words! In the planning phase of close protection operations, photos of locations, facilities, hotels, hospitals, obstacles on routes etc. can be very useful to see. If you need to set up the security for a residence, photos of the perimeter, grounds and buildings will be useful when you are briefing your team or if you are considering putting in CCTV. In protective surveillance operations, the operative should always have access to a camera to help them identify any opposition surveillance, suspicious people or vehicles among other things.

As I said earlier, photography is an invaluable skill, photos and video are used to collect, confirm, or reinforce other intelligence. At a basic level I always tell people working for me to get photos if they are visiting or watching a location to verify to the client that they have actually been there. A few years ago, we had a surveillance job on one of the Islands in the Caribbean, the target should have been there for business meetings but stayed in his 5-star hotel suite with his, let say secretary. The client doubted our story, that the target had not left his hotel room, claiming we must have been at the wrong hotel etc. but we had video of the hotel, the suite door, room service trolleys in the corridor outside the room-etc. This client had not thought about the timings for the job and would not listen to our advice so, they got what they asked for.

The best way to learn how to take decent photos and videos is to go and start taking photos and videos. These days with digital photography you don't have to worry about the cost of developing film, if you shoot 100 photos and none are any good, then delete and take another 100, it costs you nothing.

When using a camera think of it as a firearm, to get good photos or video you need to be able to aim and shoot. Always ensure when your operational that you have enough storage space and battery life on the camera, if you think you need extra make sure you have a spare memory card, battery pack and charging cables etc.

You need to know what to take photos of, but you also need to know what not to take photos of. For example, do not take unnecessary photos of team members, clients, residences or safe houses etc. Anything that could compromise an operation or leak sensitive information, always check the backgrounds of your photos, you might have something in there that you did not intend to have.

Types of photography

- **Documentation photography:** This is used to record printed documents, when doing this ensure that the print is in focus and readable.

- **Object photography:** If you need to take a photograph of an object, say a knife, try to get as much detail as possible such as markings and any serial numbers. Also, photograph the object with an object of a known size such as a pen, lighter or car key, then those viewing it can get an idea of the objects size.

- **Identification photography:** This is photographing individuals or groups of people to record their identity. The targets may or may not know that they are being photographed, an example of this would be photographing groups of protesters who may later be a potential threat. If you're taking photos of a specific individuals try to focus on faces, tattoos, scars, jewelry or shoes, anything that can be used to identify them later.

- **Location photography**: This is used to provide an overview of a location, security systems, possible surveillance sites, avenues of approach, access and exit points, vehicles on site, perimeter security etc. This maybe done covertly or overtly for defensive or offensive purposes. The main issues I have seen with location photography is that people do not take enough photos and tend to have a narrow focus instead of including wide angle or panoramic shots, which if anything interesting is identified can always be zoomed in on. A good video sweep can be worth a ton of narrow stills. When taking video footage describe what you're looking at and what direction you are looking at it from; north, east, south, west etc. This is essential as locations can look different when approached or viewed from different angles.

- **Surveillance photography:** Surveillance and counter surveillance photography is used to gather covert intelligence on individuals and locations etc. Surveillance photography usually involves some imaginative practices such as taking posed photos of individuals just to get what's going on in the background or using the selfie camera on a smartphone to get photos or video of what's going on behind you. Where there is sufficient budget remote cameras and drones can be employed.

Most private investigators or close protection operators will need to combine the principles from most of the above types of photography. For example, using photography in an advance security detail as part of a close protection operation to check out a restaurant that might be visited by a client could include:

- **Document photography:** Photos of menus and venue evacuation plans

- **Identification photography:** To record the type of crowd and key members of staff

- **Location photography:** Approach routes, overall venue, internal layout, bathrooms and exits etc.

Small details can be of great intelligence value, such as what shoes someone is wearing, what's on the screen of a person's smartphone, what the weather is like at a location, road surfaces, the flooring in a building or where the buildings water tanks are. It's always better to have more photos and video footage of the target than to be missing one critical detail. These days for surveillance it's best to take video footage as this is easier for most people and if required, stills photos can be taken from the video when editing.

When you have your photos and videos you need to save them in a secure location be it online or on a hard drive. Save the originals and edit copies if required. Ensure you save the photos in a file with a description of when and where they were taken. Photos from a route check done on a weekend afternoon may show light traffic on a road but at 08:30 on a Monday morning the same road could be congested.

I think we can all agree there is no excuse these days for someone in the private investigation or close protection industry not to have access to a camera that can take respectable photos and video.

This is only a short chapter in which I have spoken about some key points on photography for private investigators and close protection operations, I hope it gives you a few things to think about!

ATTENDING MEETINGS

Meetings can be extremely dangerous and should always be treated with caution. This is when people will know where you will be at a specific time, exactly what the bad guys want to know. Arranging meetings is an easy way to set someone up for kidnapping, assassination, sexual assault or robbery.

Meetings should be kept as secret as possible and planned well in advance. When under a high-level threat you want to exchange the maximum amount of information with those you are meeting within the shortest possible time.

Firstly, you will need to select a suitable meeting location, be it a coffee shop or a hotel suite, this will depend on how many people you'll be meeting with, what's to be discussed and what is the threat level. You should always have a reason and cover story for being in that area at that time in case the meeting is compromised; for example, maybe you or those you are meeting with have identified they are under active surveillance.

Everyone involved in the meeting will need a covert way of alerting the others that they have been followed or are under active surveillance. This can be done by using codes or signs en-route to the meeting location or quickly posted comments on online chat boards or social media sites. This way if one person is compromised, they should not compromise or endanger the rest of the participants. Cell phones should not be used or taken to sensitive meetings as they can be tracked and used as listening devices; they should also not be used to warn others that you are under surveillance, calls and text messages would lead straight to those you were meeting with. A low-tech method, such as you drinking soda instead of coffee, or putting the "Do not disturb" sign on the hotel suite door could signal the others that things have gone bad.

Whenever you are meeting people for the first time you should always use prearranged signs and countersigns to confirm their identity. The simplest thing is a pre-arranged question and answer, this works better than checking ID cards as the person you're meeting with might be the right person, but you know them by a pseudonym. In a basic context for using a pre-arranged question and answer, you want to make sure the limo driver who is meeting you at the airport is your real driver and will take you to your hotel not into months of captivity or to a garbage dump!

Considerations For Attending Meetings

• Do you know in detail the meeting location? If not, then check it or get someone trusted to check it.

• Things to take into consideration include the facilities (bathrooms, cafés, taxis, payphones, etc.), potential surveillance positions, location of surveillance cameras, escape routes.

• Will it be daylight or dark?

• What is the condition of pedestrian and vehicle traffic, what are people wearing, what's the age and type of people in the area?

• Make plans and procedures for all possible emergencies identified in your threat assessment.

• Consider where along your route to the meeting location you would put surveillance personnel to watch you if you were the opposition and identify where on your approach to the meeting location you would be channeled.

• How will you get to the meeting location: walking, using public transport or driving?

• If driving, where will you park your car, will it be secure or hidden, how long would it take you to get back to it in an emergency and what are you going to do if it's compromised?

• What will you wear for the meeting and will you need a change of clothes; remember it's always easier to dress down than up. You can always take off a sports coat and shirt and put them in a plastic bag.

• Will you be carrying any weapons and is there any risk of being searched?

• Always be aware of what's going on in the environment around you; watch for warning signs posted by the those you're meeting with that could indicate they have been compromised, any unusual activity, people waiting in cars or vans with blacked out windows, fit young men with short hair hanging around for no reason, check the body language of those waiting in possible surveillance positions, etc.

• When you reach the meeting location, sweep the area for anything suspicious, you might not be under surveillance but the person you're meeting with could be.

• If you can, select a good position at the meeting location from where you can view as many entrances as possible, be close to escape routes and view what's going on the street outside without being in clear view from outside.

• Locate those you are meeting with and exchange passwords, consider walking them to another location to identify if they are under surveillance.

• If you are going to eat and drink, consider the method of payment; credit cards leave a paper trail.

• Also, do not leave your food or drink unattended or let anyone fetch you a drink from the bar, etc. as this is an opportunity to drug it.

• Under a high threat make sure you do not leave anything behind from which fingerprints or DNA samples could be taken.

• During the meeting constantly watch for physical, video and audio surveillance, if you have the manpower get a trusted associate to do this for you and to watch your back.

• Keep the meeting as short as possible and when it's over, leave the area as quickly as possible and conduct several counter-surveillance drills, consider changing your appearance if necessary.

• If further meetings are required, they would have to be varied for different times of day and days of the week.

KIDNAP, ROBBERY, &
RAPE DRUGS

Think about how many times when you have been at a bar, club or café and left your drink unattended, for less than 10 seconds, with someone you have just met, who seemed like a nice person? That would have been more than enough time for them to spike your drink with date rape drugs such as Ketamine, GHB or Rohypnol. How often has a waiter or bartender given you an open bottle of beer or the like, which could have been spiked with illegal drugs such as Ecstasy or prescription drugs such as Xanex?

I have spent more time than most in bars in developing countries and I can't remember being served a can of beer, bottle of beer or a bottle of liquor that was not opened in front of me. The main reason is so the bars' patrons know they are getting what they ordered and not a cheaper brand of alcohol that has just been poured into a quality brand name bottle. This from a security perspective also makes it harder for the drinks to be spiked by the bar staff and waiters. I tend to avoid drinking draft beers or shots unless I can see the drinks being poured, to me that's not being paranoid its being careful!

At this time, I am living in South Florida and hear regular stories of males and females having their drinks spiked in bars and clubs with date rape drugs. The motive is commonly thought of as "Date Rape" but this criminal tactic is also used in robberies. There has been a change in rapist and criminal tactics where many have gone over to using prescription drugs which are widely available, especially in South Florida, as from a legal standpoint its more difficult for the victims to argue they were drugged and not taking the drugs by their own accord. This is a common defense of not only the rapists and criminals but also the venues where people have initially been drugged.

Rapists target males and females alike and in addition to the physical injuries of the assault there are also the issues of pregnancies and sexually transmitted diseases. Not only are drugs used for sexual assaults but also robberies.

Back in the 1990s when I was doing business in Eastern Europe there was one nightclub in Riga, Latvia where it was common knowledge that visitors who flashed their money and Rolexes around could end up drugged and robbed, they would wake up in the morning somewhere missing their valuables. When they reported the robberies to the police, they would not take the victims seriously, what was to prove they did not drink themselves unconscious, the victim could not remember what they were doing, so they could have given their valuables away etc. As long as no one got hurt the police in Riga weren't concerned.

In South Florida it's common for men to meet a woman at a bar to have their drink spiked and be robbed of their luxury watches, jewelry and wallets. And if they manage to make it home before passing out, they tend to lose a lot more. These crimes are regularly reported, and I expect a lot more are not.

You don't have to go to bars and nightclubs to be exposed to the risk of being drugged, one Gypsy tactic in Europe is to get their small children to go out and sell glasses of tea or soft drinks to tourists. Who would expect a little girl to give you a spiked drink? The children are accompanied by teenagers who then watch and follow the victims until they pass out or start to stumble, at which time they rob them.

A drug that is regularly used in crimes in Colombia, Venezuela and Ecuador is Burandanga or Scopolamine which is extracted from the Borrachero tree. Scopolamine has numerous legitimate medical uses, but when used by rapists and criminals it renders their victims into a compliant zombie like state of which they remember nothing. Victims have the outward appearance of being okay but are in fact in a trance and know nothing of what they're doing.

Victims of Scopolamine overdoses are common in Colombian hospitals as are the deaths of those who received a large dose or had a low tolerance. This drug is more common than people think and is out there, I have come across similar drugs in Haiti and West Africa, once administered through liquid or powder form the victim is completely compliant and helpless.

The common date rape drugs like Rohypnol, GHB, Ketamine are tasteless and odorless and take approximately 15 to 30 minutes to take effect and usually last from three to six hours, depending on dosage. These drugs make the victims weak, making them unconscious and unable to remember what happened. Prescription drugs such as Klonopin and Xanax have similar effects, all of which are enhanced when the victim had been drinking alcohol.

If you are out at a bar, club or just accepted a drink from a stranger and start to feel weak or dizzy for no apparent reason get help immediately. Get to a safe location, get to trusted friends, call your friends or family, even call an ambulance but do not go with strangers!

This is only a short article but hopefully you can see it's better to be careful and thought paranoid than it is to end up drugged, kidnapped, abused and dumped in the gutter!

THE SEX BUSINESS – A GATEWAY
TO BLACKMAIL & EXTORTION

It always surprises me how many guys who claim to be players don't understand the sex business and end up in trouble because they get duped by girls using routines and scams that have been around since women realized how dumb guys were. It amazes me as a security professional how many guys get themselves into situations that can damage their health, safety and professional reputation by being stupid. So, here are some words of advice and warning from someone who understands how things work!

Looking back, I was very lucky at being exposed to the realities of the sex business in my late teens while serving in the British Army in Cyprus. I was in an Infantry unit and after a two-year tour of Northern Ireland we were posted to the Mediterranean Island for two years, which with its abundance of cabaret clubs proved to be a very good training ground for an inquisitive 19-year-old squaddie.

Like in most places the cabaret clubs and prostitution business in Cyprus is a Mafia run business, at the time the working girls were from mainly Asia with some Eastern Europeans. Were they the victims of sex trafficking; I am sure they were making more money as hookers in Cyprus than they would in their own countries, business is business. To be honest I never heard of our guys being scammed by the girls, but we were just young soldiers with little to offer and nothing to lose. For most of us the novelty quickly wore off as the abundance of tourists meant getting laid was not a problem and the polite girls even paid for the drinks.

But boys will be boys, and we had those that fell in love with these working girls. As I remember several of the guys who were spotted much too regularly in the cabarets even went to the Philippines Embassy in Nicosia to try to help the girls get a ticket home. I am sure the girls were just playing the sympathy card for some extra cash or hoping these naïve young men with British Passports would marry them and give them access to the European Union. I bet if the girls knew what the guys whose virginity they took were doing to help them they would not have been very happy. I am sure they really wanted to be deported back to where they come from and have to explain to the businessmen who arranged their flights, visas and employment how they were going to pay their debt off.

It's a fact of life that people have vices and I do not judge people on what they do in private, as long as it is between consenting adults. I discuss the sex business with my clients as it's an area where unwary people can and do get themselves into a lot of trouble. One example of an avoidable problem was the situation the U.S. Secret Service had in Cartagena, Colombia, which was absolutely ridiculous on many levels.

The most common and accepted side of the sex industry are the strip bars and they can be found in most places, some are very classy and well-run businesses, but many are not. During the late 90's I had more than a few business meetings in strip clubs in central, eastern Europe and also supplied security for several clubs in London, so I know a little bit about how things work. You need to understand this basic fact, as soon as you walk through the door you are a commodity.

The sex business is a business, it's all about hard currency, so forget the emotions. Remember you're paying for the show, you're paying for attention, and the working girls are just doing their job as long as you're paying. Strip bars should be thought of as the same way you think about a patisserie. You go, select your cake, buy it, enjoy it and move on until next time. Many times, in Eastern Europe I have seen the drunk businessman trying to dance while surrounded by two or three hot young women; if he has the money and he wants them they are his, for a few hours or the night at least.

Hopefully before the gentleman leaves the club either alone or with the girl who's within his price range, he has avoided some of the common issues with strip bars and clip joints. A typical scam is to vastly overcharge for drinks, when the bill is presented our gent finds out his couple of beers cost a few hundred dollars. When he protests he is confronted by a couple of thugs who shows him the price list for drinks, which is well-hidden behind the bar. In most cases he will have his wallet emptied and may be escorted to an ATM machine and instructed to draw out more money or just beaten and robbed. If the gentleman is with friends, one may be held in the venue while the other is sent to get more money. These operations rely on the fact that the people going into these places will not report these incidents to the police as they don't want people, such as their wives and bosses to know that they were in a sleazy strip bar in the first place.

It was common in Eastern Europe for those who flashed money and jewelry around in the clubs to end up drugged and robbed, their drinks being spiked by the bar staff or those they were social-izing with. If they reported the robberies to the police they would not be taken seriously, what was to prove they did not drink them-selves unconscious, they could not remember what they were doing, so they could have given their valuables away etc.

The threat from violence is also always present, be it from the jealous guy who's infatuated with the girl that's giving you all the attention tonight or the wannabe gangster that see's you as an easy source of a few dollars. Most of the working girls are also more than capable of hurting more than your feelings, don't be surprised if the pretty young thing who took your wallet defends her honor by putting a glass in your face; now explain that to your wife after the bouncers finish throwing you out.

In most places prostitution is illegal but in some places, it is a licensed business and even where it's illegal, you will not have to look far to find sex for sale. In Eastern Europe it's not uncommon to get hookers phoning your hotel room offering their services; your details supplied by their associates working in the hotel. Or the hotel concierge can arrange girls for you, maybe for a fee but be assured everyone is making a percentage of any deals that the prostitute makes with you.

Whether the hookers are found online, at a strip bar or supplied by other sources they can all bring big problems, not only disease but also robbery and blackmail. If the hooker has friends in the hotel, they can access your hotel registration details, which will more than likely include your home address, business address and credit card details. How much would most men pay to stop the photos or video from their hotel's security cameras showing him and a young lady getting cozy in the hotel bar, and then going to his room, being sent to his wife? Get the picture?

I have heard quite a few stories of men taking hookers to their business and their homes when their families are not there because they are too cheap to get a hotel room, I usually hear the stories when they start to be extorted. The U.S. secret service agents in Cartagena, Colombia were stupid enough to take hookers to their hotel rooms where they had their weapons, presidential security plans, phones and computers etc. There are plenty of "by the hour" hotels in Colombia, so why take a hooker to your hotel, the less your new friend knows about you the better, even if you are in love!

5 Star hotels and exclusive venues are always a favored hangout for attractive women seeking to better themselves and make some hard currency in the process. Be it London, Paris, Miami or Port Harcourt these ladies will not be hard to find. One funny story involves a gentleman I know who exchanged phone numbers with a very attractive lady he met in a high-end hotel lobby in Abuja in Nigeria. After an evening exchanging texts, he invited a girl to his

hotel room. When she got to his hotel room an argument quickly broke out as he did not realize he had to pay for her time, I think his ego was hurt. He ended up paying the girl, which was the right thing to do, he was dumb and had wasted her time, for her it was business, if he just wanted a conversation he should have Skyped his wife.

As I said in the beginning, a lot of the sex business is run by organized crime to some extent and in a lot of places the police provide protection for the venues and the girls. With a call to her friends in the police, our dumb friend's actions in Abuja could have caused him a lot of third world problems which would have cost him a lot more than the girl's fee to make go away.

While providing security for high-end events in London's West End I have had numerous arguments with very well dressed, attractive young ladies trying to gatecrash exclusive events. At one very stuffy black-tie event two stunning girls managed to bypass security by paying the £500.00 each for tickets for the event, and at the rate they were giving out business cards I am sure they made a profit on their investment that night alone.

For the high-end and well-connected girls when not socializing or on call in exclusive venues, they tend to work from apartments in usually very nice parts of town. And for those that can afford them they are a far safer bet than the girls that you will encounter at the strip bars. For the starting fee of $1000.00 for an evening of conversation with the option to negotiate for sexual favors you should also secure maximum discretion. But be assured the girls and their employers have taken their precautions, these days usually in the form of their apartments being equipped with covert cameras which are monitored by a close at hand minder. Remember; an incriminating video is a lot harder to explain away than a few cuts and bruises, right?

But I am sure most of these city gents and dapper Casanovas who as far as their wives are concerned are socializing at their old boys' club, have only honorable intentions. What's more honorable than a quick haircut at Harrods and a couple of hours with two girls of your choice who are there to please. Hopefully it never occurred to these gents that 45 minutes before they turned up, some with flowers and some without, that the girls had been servicing someone else. And hopefully for their egos sake if it was not their first visit the girls actually remembered them, a good reason to tip well or be a real kink eh!

If you miss the warning signs and are set up, "honey trapped", your world can quickly go from extreme ecstasy to extreme misery. At the low end of the scale that hot chick that promises you a night of debauchery will just take you to a shady hotel room or apartment where you'll be beaten, robbed and maybe raped by her waiting accomplices. An imaginative honey trap happened to a French businessman in 2002. He met an attractive Russian girl online and agreed to meet her in Moscow. She met him at Sheremetyevo airport and took him to a waiting car where he was kidnapped! The first his wife knew about him going to Moscow was when she received a ransom demand for $3,000,000.00. His kidnappers were not professional, and he was rescued by the Moscow police. This case made the international media, so how much damage it did it do to his credibility? Not to mention how he would explain the situation to his wife.

At a higher level a more intricate honey trap can go on for an extended period of time until you believe it's some form of relationship, of course the sex, the more deviant the better would be videoed and then used to blackmail you for business favors or hard currency. A common criminal tactic is to pimp out a girl or boy who looks the legal consenting age for sex and then claim after the sex has taken place, they are underage. That way they have a lot of leverage on the unfortunate and stupid gent who has without knowing possibly committed a serious criminal act, sex with a minor.

I do not judge others' lifestyles; I have been fortunate to experience a lot of what the world has to offer, I understand how things work and see a lot of things a lot differently than most. I tell my clients not to get into situations and environments they do not understand because things can go very wrong, very quickly. Especially in the world of the sex business, be it legal or illegal. In many cases if things go bad the police will not be interested in helping you, even if you can report the crime without being implicated in illegal activities yourself.

Always remember what I said earlier, the sex business is a business, it's all about hard currency not emotions and you are the commodity.

SEXTORTION – ONLINE EXTORTION

Sextortion is a scam that is becoming more and more common with those that like to send sexual or nude selfies etc. to strangers and supposed friends... No only can this effect someone's personal life but also the reputation of the company they are working for. There have been plenty of sex scandals making the news this year, so from a management point of view keep your people informed and let them know the consequences of sharing sexy photos online or via their phones!!!

Sextortion is a crime they are having big problems within Europe. An old friend of mine from the British Army who is now a British Police Detective was explaining they are receiving a lot of calls from people who have been caught out by this scam.

This is how things usually develop: the scammer will set up a social media profile of an attractive young girl or boy and then start sending out friend requests to likely looking victims. When someone accepts their friend request, they start to politely message then build up a virtual relationship over say a few weeks. When they feel the victim is comfortable with them, they start sending nude and sexual photos or videos and asking the same in return.

When the scammers have sufficient videos and photos of the victim then the extortion begins. The threat is usually for a relatively small amount of money, £250.00 GBP; why so small, because this is an amount most can afford, however it is a lot of money in say Nigeria. If the victim refuses to pay, then the scammers tell them that they have or had access to their friends and contacts list and will send their sexual photos and videos out to everyone.

For most people this would cause a lot of embarrassment, for those with work colleagues, bosses or employers on their social media it could cost them their job. I am quite sure the vast majority of these cases are not reported to the police and the victims pay up.

This scam is also very prevalent in the Middle East and Central Asia where the cultures are very conservative. The scammers target these cultures because they know if they make public a sexually explicit video, of say someone from Saudi Arabia for example, that person could end up in a lot of legal problems. In many Central Asian cultures, it would lead to the person being disowned by their family or in the case of a female, an honor killing.

So, while sexting can appear to be just harmless fun, it can generate a lot of negative repercussions ranging from embarrassment, loss of friends, lawsuits, criminal complaints, extortion and suicides.

How can all this be prevented? Very simply... Do not let people you don't know or trust into your social media networks, and if you need to let in work colleagues or others whom you don't know, then be careful what you post, and set up another personal profile just for close friends.

Also, the golden rule, do not send or post anything that you are not comfortable with being made public!

INTERVIEWS & DEBRIEFS

A major part of investigations and intelligence operations is the interviewing of witnesses and debriefing of informants. One of the differences between the interviewing of witnesses and debriefing of informants is that a witness might need to go to court to give evidence, whereas an informant is supplying confidential information.

Evidence presented in court, must be verified by a witness and their statements must have been taken in a professional environment to a set format. Debriefing an informant might consist of a quick conversation in a bar where you record the conversation on your smartphone so you can go over and process it later on.

In this chapter, I am going to briefly go over what you need to consider when interviewing or debriefing someone. I am not going to talk about taking formal witness statements as the requirements vary from country to country due to their individual laws. Wherever you are operating if you need to take a formal statement from someone ensure it's in full compliance with the local laws.

Over the years I have been interviewed and debriefed in numerous settings and for various reasons and I find it funny how many of those doing the questioning follow standard textbook procedures. I have had people play good guy and bad guy, repeatedly ask the same questions trying to catch me out, use sleep deprivation and of course make extreme threats. I have even had people put obscure theories into the conversation that I know could have only come from specific people that were telling tales on me, thank you very much btw!

If you're the one being questioned stick to your story, or cover story, but remember: if a story is repeated perfectly word for word, chances are that a professional interrogator will know it's been rehearsed!

As I have said throughout this book, intelligence and counter-intelligence are two sides of the same coin. You can employ the tactics and techniques against others and can expect others to employ them against you. You must think outside the box, because if you're dealing with professionals, they will already know the textbook tactics and responses.

The Basics

As soon as the witness or informant decides to talk to you, they could be putting your and their lives at risk. You need to consider all risks to yourself and the person you're intending to talk to and do everything possible to minimize them. Not only is there the risk of physical violence but also the risk of compromising investigations, operations and the destruction of evidence.

When interviewing and debriefing you must remain professional and impartial. To get the best results, the person you're talking with must be comfortable with you and believe that you are not judging them or their actions. Many witnesses and informants will be very afraid, and you will need to reassure them that they are safe, and you are working in their interests.

You need to be very careful when dealing with scared and vulnerable people to ensure that they are not just telling you what they think you want to hear. They need to know that you want them to only tell you the facts and if they don't have the answers to your questions, they will not be punished in anyway. On the other hand, they need to understand that if they lie, give you disinformation or hold back on information they will be squeezed in some way.

The location for the interview or the debrief can also influence how the person you're talking to behaves. If you want to make someone comfortable meet them in an environment they are used to, keep them in their comfort zone. If you want to apply pressure on someone then take them to a location, you know will be outside of their comfort zone.

Before the interview or debriefing you need to have a strategy and your questions pre-planned. If necessary, select trusted others to conduct the interview if you believe they would have a better rapport with the witness or informant than yourself. If you're using multiple interviewers make sure they know who will be taking the lead in the questioning and what topics they need to concentrate on specifically. The interviewers would need to be briefed on the objectives and the background of the operation and debriefed after they have spoken with the witness or informant. Things that you need to consider before you talk with a witness or informant are:

• **Their age:** Knowing the person's age helps to determine the best individual to interview them, an older person might have no rapport or respect for someone half their age for example.

• **Cultural background:** The interviewer must understand the culture of the person they are talking to.

• **Religion:** People's religious beliefs need to be understood and respected.

• **Gender:** Straight, gay, transgender... You don't want a homophobe interviewing a person who is transgender...

• **Personal life:** Are they married, single, gay, have children, cheating on their partners, etc.?

• **Physical and mental health:** This needs to be taken into consideration for their safety and possibly yours.

• **Previous contact:** Is the person known and could they be a security threat? Could the meeting be a set up for an assault?

Questioning

The first step to questioning someone is to get them talking, this is where some knowledge of their personal life and interests helps. Where time allows, the initial conversation does not have to be about the investigation or operation, some small talk can help to relax the witness or informant. When you start talking business then make sure the witness or informant knows that you want the facts only, and that you are impartial and are there to help them when you can.

The witness or informant needs to understand why you want to talk to them. The reason, real or not, should have been worked out in the planning phase and the initial questions need to be about that reason. As the interview develops you can take the conversation in the direction that you require. The witness or informant needs to know you are interested in knowing anything that they feel could be relevant, such as the personal lives, circumstances and opinions of others involved in the investigation or operation. You need to let the witness or informant talk; as they talk, they will relax and will become more comfortable with you. Consider:

• Is your body language giving the right impression?

• Always allow the person you're talking to pause and think, without interrupting.

• Encouraging the person to talk until they have given the full story.

• Guide the witness or informant in the direction you want and try to emphasize important topics.

• Go back and bring up previously talked about topics to clarify and expand on what's already been said.

• Ensure you covered to the best of your ability the questions and topics you identified in your interview plan.

Your questions should have been pre-planned and must be put across in language that the witness or informant understands. Keep your questions short, simple and to the point. Do not over-complicate the language you use or the questions as this can confuse the person you're talking to. You can expand and clarify what the person is saying by using various pre-planned questions and responses. Types of questions include:

• **Open-ended:** For example, saying 'Tell me', 'Describe' or 'Explain' invites the person to expand on what they have said and talk freely.

• **Specific-closed:** Questions such as 'Who shot him?' 'What did he say?' or 'Where do they stay?' can be used to clarify the specifics of what the person is saying or could be reluctant to say. Such questions are best asked when the conversation is warmed up, since they can come across as too direct if the person you are talking to is scared or nervous.

• **Forced-choice:** 'Were the drugs sold or exchanged?', these types of questions can lead to the person guessing the answer and are best used when you know the answer but want to see if the person is lying or ill-informed.

• **Multiple:** Asking questions such as 'Where did they come from, what did they do, where did they go to?' can confuse the person you're talking to. Keep questions short, simple and to the point.

• **Leading:** Saying such things as 'You saw the knife, right?' can lead the witness or informant to give you an answer they think you are asking for. Leading questions are less credible and should only be used when finally confirming previous statements.

Where time allows you should try to summarize what's been said before closing up the conversation and ensure the witness or informant has nothing else to say and you have asked all your questions. Once the interview or debrief is over, what's been said needs to be processed and a decision made if further actions or meetings are required.

Types Of People And Hints For Interviewing

• **Talkative:** Let them talk; listen and select what you require.

• **Reluctant:** This is the person who does not want to talk. Either they do not like publicity, they dislike you or be a friend of the ones you're after. You need to understand them and gain their confidence and assure them you can work together.

• **Emotional:** This person can easily confuse what they have seen, heard or imagined. Always verify their stories and beware that they are not just seeking attention.

• **Timid:** This type of person can prove to be a valuable and reliable witness; be friendly and encourage them to talk.

• **Hysterical:** Do not question them. Calm them down and get back to them later if necessary.

• **Shy and Nervous:** Dealing with them can take patience and understanding. Be friendly, build a rapport and don't pressure.

• **Adolescent:** Normally self-centered, worst observers and rarely describe accurately what they see or hear. Always double check their stories.

• **Middle-Aged:** People in this age group generally have fixed viewpoints and prejudices; this is where knowing their backgrounds helps to build a rapport.

• **Elderly:** Elderly people can be keen observers, but they may need to be kept focused.

• **Lying:** Check and re-check their stories. They can be used for spreading disinformation or exposed and then, have pressure applied so that they tell the truth.

Recording Interviews And Debriefs

These days everything should be recorded where possible if the circumstances and threat level allow. Do not record and save anything that could compromise a witness or informant. Remember that recorded statements, especially virtual, when used as evidence can always be deemed as non-credible due to the fact, they have been recorded in a non-professional environment. Witnesses and informants can always claim they were intimidated or blatantly lying. Statements need to always be backed up with facts and evidence.

BEING ARRESTED

I find it amusing that in the close protection and investigations industry these days everyone is trying to be the squeaky clean perfect little protectors and detectives, which is all well and good, to some extent as long as nothing goes wrong and the clients are behaving. The issue is when things do go wrong and get heated, which they do often, you need people around you that are street wise and have a spine, not choir boys who are going to sing and cause more problems for everyone involved.

These days if you travel internationally, if you are going to be working in the emerging markets or are just not liked in some circles then you are running the risk of being arrested for some reason. Criminals are not the only ones who can end up in hand-cuffs! It may come as a shock to some people, but many police forces are corrupt and not just in the emerging markets.

I have experienced both police and state corruption in Western Europe and the U.S.; just because someone has a badge, it does not mean they are honest and trustworthy. Many people, particularly those who are not well traveled, are suspicious of strangers, especially if the stranger is a foreigner. If you are seen acting suspiciously, talking about security matters and taking pictures of venues, you could be taken for a spy or a terrorist and arrested.

In many places if the local police find out you are providing close protection or investigation services, you're going to get hassled… Identification, Licenses and weapons permits will be checked to start with. Why? Usually for no other reason than the cops are bored or jealous. If you're providing close protection services, the cops can mess with you in front of your client and then drop their business cards to the client in the hope of getting some off-duty work. Be assured if they find the slightest reason to detain or arrest you, they will, and if you are in 3rd world countries, things can be a lot worse!

A simple example I can give was that I was once traveling with a group of people through Italy in the early 1990's, at one port on the Adriatic several of the group members decided to wander off and take some photos of some Italian navy patrol boats. By the time I had located them they had been taken on board one of the vessels and were being questioned by the military police. They handed over their film, explained they were tourists, the police were very professional, and everyone went on their way, but in some countries taking photos of anything military related can get you into a lot of trouble.

If you are ever involved in a violent confrontation and end up hurting or killing someone, you will be arrested. If you are a foreigner, the chances will be that the local authorities will be against you to start with, and they'll want to make an example of you. Especially if they find out you're a bodyguard, investigator or security contractor etc.

You need to make plans for what to do in this situation; you don't want to end up in a 3rd world prison because you took a gun off, and shot a kidnapper, who turned out to be a police officer. In many countries, even developed Western countries, since 9/11, the mere fact that you are a foreigner will put you in the same league as a terrorist in many people's minds. Unfortunately, it will mean nothing if you are a 100% law-abiding citizen.

You must also remember; the most dangerous time will be the first few minutes of your arrest. You can expect some level of violence, even from police in 1st world countries. In the US most cops first response to an incident is to draw their guns, if they see any possible threat, they shoot, so be very careful especially when dealing with armed, nervous and scared police.

If you're providing serious security or investigative services you must always keep a low profile, have an escape plan including several routes to a safe location and know how to get out of the country. Also, have protocols in place for if you, your client or team members are arrested or detained by the police, military or government agencies...

Being Arrested

Below are some basic considerations on what to do if your detained or arrested. What you say and do depends on where you are, the situation, and the attitude of the police... Just remember in many locations the local police are not paid that well and will welcome donations to their welfare funds etc.

• **Protocols:** You need to have a plan in place and all team members need to know it. At a basic level everyone needs to know how to alert other team members that they have a potential legal problem with the police. A simple coded text message to team members who are not at the arrest location alerting them there is a problem can be enough to get the ball rolling. If additional details can be supplied such as the exact location of the arrest, details of the arresting police unit, a reason for the arrest it can help with the response to the incident.

• **Being Arrested:** When you are being detained or arrested remain calm and try to clarify why you are being detained or arrested if it is not clear. Be very careful what you say as one wrong word or aggressive statement can land you in a lot more trouble. If you are being transported to a police station or jail, try to inform other team members who are not directly involved so they know where you are.

• **Know Your Rights:** Part of your pre-planning needs to be researching the basic laws of the location you are visiting or staying in. You need to understand what your rights are if you are arrested such as, how long can you be detained before being charged, will you have access to a lawyer, who will pay for the lawyer, will your embassy be informed, will you be allowed to make phone calls, do you have the numbers of those you need to call if you don't have access to your phone?

• **False Information:** You need to be very suspicious of any unverifiable information given to you by the police, other inmates and even lawyers. Any unverifiable information could be false information that is being given to you to entrap you or to get you to sign a confession etc.

• **Documents and Translations:** Never sign documents that you do not understand! If possible, get your own trusted lawyer and translator. Lawyers and translators supplied by the local police etc. may not be working in your favor or translating questions and documents incorrectly.

• **Being Charged:** If you are formally charged and given a court date you will need a decent lawyer who should try to get you released on bail or house arrest as soon as possible.

• **Questioned Under Duress:** You can take it for granted the police will try to intimidate you into giving false statements, signing documents and in many places will ignore your legal rights. All you can do in these situations is stick to your story, protocols and wait for those you are working with to arrange the proper lawyers and legal support. If you are assaulted or tortured try to keep a record of your injuries, medical attention that you required and hospital visits etc.

• **Documentation and Evidence:** If you or your team have documentation, photos, videos or other evidence you need to keep it secure. At the time of the arrest do everything possible to share evidence with those not directly involved in the incident. If you have photos and videos on your smart phones and they are seized by the police, the evidence will be lost, or the phones will disappear. Consider having all photos, videos and documents on operational phones automatically synchronized and backed up to a cloud storage account that other team members and trusted associates have access to.

• **Jail:** Even in 1st world countries jails are very dangerous places and those not used to such environments can suffer intimidation, violence and sexual assault. Personal security and safety must be your priority, and everything from hygiene to receiving proper food must be considered. This is where support from team members is essential so you can be sent food and supplies, or money to purchase food and supplies. Even though violence is common in many jails be very careful if you're involved in any hostile situations as not to inflict excessive injuries on any opponents, as you could end up being charged with additional crimes. If possible, try to make friends with respected prisoners who could help you avoid potential issues with other prisoners or guards.

• **Support Groups:** Alerting political contacts, charities and community groups can raise awareness and support. In some cases, the intervention of local or foreign political representatives can speed up cases going to court and lead to the early release of prisoners.

• **Media:** The media is a double-edged blade; it can work for you and against you. Trusted media contacts can help raise awareness of your arrest, which might prevent you from disappearing completely... But information and interviews given to unreliable media outlets can be edited and spun against you! Try to ensure that media reports that are given in your favor do not criticize the police, judges or government of the country in which you were arrested and detained in.

From this short chapter hopefully, I have made it clear that you do not want to get arrested! As part of your basic planning you should have worked out your protocols on what to do if involved in an incident that could lead to a team member, or the clients arrest. If you listen to the advice from most embassies, they will tell you to contact and cooperate with the local police if you are involved in a confrontation etc. Well, my advice would be that it may make more sense, and save a lot of trouble and money, just to get out of the area or country as quickly and discreetly as possible.

INTERROGATION

If you travel internationally or are going to be working in the emerging markets, you are running the risk of being kidnapped or arrested for some reason. The most dangerous time during an arrest or kidnapping will be the first ten to fifteen minutes. You can expect some level of violence, even from police in 1st world countries.

Kidnappers will need to show they are in control of the situation and will be happy to bust a few of your ribs to stop you from resisting. You can expect to be handcuffed, with your hands behind your back, searched and blindfolded. You will then probably be taken to a place where you will be interrogated or kept. If you are taken by vehicle, you may be placed face down in the back seat or in the trunk.

When you reach the area where you will be interrogated, such as a police station, farm outbuilding or basement, you can expect to be strip searched. If your abductors are professional, they will operate in silence, and you will not see their faces or anything that you could use to later identify them. After the strip search, you may be left naked or given clothes to wear, if the abductors are professional, you will be left naked. The reason for the strip search and the confiscation of your clothes is to make sure that you do not have any escape equipment hidden on you. Also, most people will feel embarrassed and vulnerable when they are naked in front of strangers and it also makes escaping more difficult, imagine having to run cross country through bushes naked!

You can now expect to be kept naked, handcuffed blindfolded and in isolation and if you're interrogators are professional, you will be placed in a stress position. This will be a position which will be very painful and uncomfortable for you to maintain, however, if you do not maintain this position, you will most probably be hurt in some way. You can be left in stress positions for anywhere from two to twenty-four hours and the only contact you will have with your abductors will be painful for you.

How your interrogation progresses will depend upon who you are dealing with and what information they are after, if anything specific at all. Are they after information on your business associates' locations, or do they want you to sign a statement admitting to a crime? You will be made generous offers by your interrogators for complying with their wishes and threats if you don't. What you do and how you handle the situation is up to you, if the interrogators are professionals, they will make you talk. This is where again, you need to sit down and work out procedures for how you would deal with this situation. If your kidnappers are after information on your colleagues or family members have a cover story ready but remember, if a story is repeated too consistently a professional interrogator will know it's been rehearsed!

Methods Of Interrogation

A professional interrogator's main objective is to get information from a hostage and will employ various techniques to do so. The main thing they will be trying to do is mentally break the hostage down, so they will comply with the interrogator's requests. To start with, the reason why professionals will keep their hostages naked is because this puts most people at a psychological disadvantage to start with, it's all about mind games!

The methods of interrogation can be broken down into three categories: physical, sensory deprivation and chemical. Most interrogators will use a combination of physical stress and sensory deprivation.

Physical Interrogation

To put it simply, physical methods of interrogation involve inflicting pain and putting the hostage under physical stress. There are thousands of ways of inflicting pain on someone, some are quite sophisticated, but most are barbaric. The problem with this form of interrogation is that the interrogators need to be very careful not to kill the hostage before they get the information they want from them. Some people have a higher tolerance for pain and this method of interrogation will not work. It is also proven that people are more willing to give false information when being tortured, just a stop the pain. Most of the methods used will also leave marks on the hostage, such as bruises, cuts, missing body parts etc. This will not present a positive image of the terrorist group or police department, if the hostage or prisoner appears on a news report or in court badly beaten or on crutches.

The use of water to simulate drowning is a commonly used technique. The advantage of simulated drowning is that it does not leave any marks on the hostage, an enhance version of this is to substitute the water for other substances such as fizzy drinks, hot sauce or gasoline.

Sexual assaults against males and females can also be employed by unscrupulous interrogators. During the civil wars and revolutions in Latin America during the 1960's to 1990's glass Coca-Cola bottles were used to sexually assault prisoner's and hostages. One of the reasons for Coca-Cola bottle's being used is psychological, as advertising for the product is everywhere; what do you think the released prisoner will be thinking about every time they see a TV or billboard ad for Coca-Cola?

Brutal physical interrogation techniques are not employed by what I would class as professional interrogators; there is no need. If you are dealing with a situation where someone has been kidnapped and is being tortured, the odds are they are not going to be released alive.

Sensory Deprivation

This is the main method of interrogation used by professional interrogators and is proven to get the best results from those being questioned. In general, people in developed countries are very weak due to the comfortable lives they live. All their lives they eat at least three or more good meals a day; they get plenty of sleep and the last time that many experienced violence was in the school yard. For many, their experience of being cold is when the heating breaks down in their cars. Fact: most people are soft.

I have described what will happen when you are abducted or arrested, now consider this. A well-off businessman is naked, in a stress position, blindfolded, handcuffed and has received a bit of a beating. He is very scared, confused and in pain. He will be left in various stress positions for at least twenty-four hours. His captors can place small bits of glass, gravel or drawing pins on the floor, so when he falls because he can no longer stay in the stress position, these will cut him and cause a small amount of pain; his pain can be increased by putting surgical spirit or aftershave into the cuts, which will also help keep the cuts clean. In a short time, he will understand that the small amount of pain of the stress position is better than the pain that will result from falling.

Every now and again, the guard may kick his feet away from under him, just to keep him on edge. The room he is in can be cold, with a few inches of water on the floor and there can be a radio playing loud white noise. The hostage will be very scared, confused, disorientated and stressed. Most people have never gone twenty-four hours without sleep in their lives and, when they are forced to do so, they find it extremely difficult. After twenty-four hours without sleep and being forced to stay in stress positions, the hostage will be interrogated, and he will be a different person to the one who was abducted. After forty-eight hours without sleep, food, or the use of a toilet, the hostage will be in a bad way. This treatment can go on indefinitely.

Alternatively, he could also be placed in a small hot and dark room, and every half an hour or so, could have cold water thrown over him, be kicked or shot with a BB gun to prevent him from sleeping and to keep him on edge. This goes on for twenty-four hours; then he would be fed for the first time. The food could be of very poor quality or of a good quality but very salty or spicy, designed to make him thirsty or it could even be laced with a laxative to give him diarrhea. Water could be tightly rationed or again laced with something to make it taste bad. After seventy-two hours, he will be in a very bad way having gone without sleep, been hot, in pain and covered in his own body waste.

He would then be interrogated and, all going well, after the interrogation, he may be hosed down, handcuffed with his hands in the front, be allowed to sleep for a while and be given something decent to eat and drink; this will seem like heaven to him. At the next interrogation, if he does not, please the interrogators, all these privileges can be taken away and he'll be back into the old routine. This scenario can go on indefinitely and would put the hostage under extreme psychological pressure, if used over extended periods of time this treatment would do permanent damage to the hostage's mental health.

Chemical Interrogation

This form of interrogation involves the hostage being given various drugs, which can cause the prisoner to relax, hallucinate or make the body become very sensitive to the slightest touch. This form of interrogation is usually only used by government type agencies as a last resort and is barred under the Geneva Convention. Although I have never heard of any examples of criminals and terrorists using chemicals during interrogations, I am sure it would not be hard for them to get the required drugs and the people with the skill to mix and administer them. If the drugs were used by professional interrogators in conjunction with some of the other techniques, we have mentioned I can see them being very effective. If you ever have to face this type of interrogation, I hope whatever you were doing was financially worth it; I would not expect you to live to spend the money, though.

Conclusion

How you handle the interrogation will depend on you, who's interrogating you and the reason why you are being interrogated. There is no magic advice to give on how to withstand being interrogated by professionals or amateurs. If you are dealing with professionals, they will make you talk; if you are dealing with amateurs, things may get messy. Your goal will be to do whatever you have to do to survive, that's it!

ESCAPE & EVASION

Here are some basic instructions on how to avoid getting captured if you manage to escape from your kidnappers or from a location where things have gone very wrong. We do not encourage people to break the law, but you must understand that in some situations what would be viewed as illegal actions, such as breaking and entering into a building or stealing supplies, are your only option for survival.

Fundamentals Of Otr (On The Run)

Part of your SHTF plan needs to be what to do if you have to escape from a hostile situation, be it urban or rural, and be it in your local area, or somewhere you're visiting or doing business. Always ensure you have the basic equipment required to navigate and sustain yourself in the environment you're in, keep it basic, keep it light and keep it concealable.

• Your goal is survival and to reach a safe area.

• If you have a cell phone on you, then consider if those after you can use it to track you. If those after you have access to the phone company's networks dump the phone completely.

• Consider your means of leaving the area: on foot, swimming, using public transport, aircraft, boat, hitch a lift, steal or hijack a vehicle.

• After the initial escape try to leave the area as quickly as possible and keep a low profile, remember to blend in with your environment.

• As soon as you can, you need to make contact with friends, family, trusted authorities or friendly Embassies.

• If you cannot leave the area then you'll have to go to ground and hide, locations can include such places as parks or in bushes, busy pedestrian areas, public bathrooms, bars and night clubs etc. Consider what CCTV is in the area and if those after you can access it. If you're hiding in parks etc. do those who are looking for you have thermal imaging equipment? Consider how long you will have to go to ground for, and what are your emergency escape routes.

• Work out where are you running to and try to leave decoys pointing to different locations; book a train ticket with your credit card but never take a train etc.

• You will need money, if you are very lucky and have a credit card hidden on your person, you can use ATM's but remember this will show you location. If you are in an area where you're staying for a while, you could possibly have previously stashed cash with other important documents and equipment in a dead drop for emergencies. Your last resort would be to steal money.

• You will also need clean clothes, if you cannot buy them or get them from a place of charity you would need to steal them.

• If you need to travel a long distance you will need to find somewhere to wash and stay clean.

• You will need somewhere to sleep; in urban environments it may make sense to stay away from the usual places homeless people congregate as this would be the first place those looking for you would check.

• If you do not have money to buy food you could possibly get it from charities, steal it or check the trash cans behind restaurants and sandwich shops.

• To leave most countries you will need a passport or ID, if you have lost yours, you can try to covertly bypass border controls and then make it to the nearest friendly Embassy on the other side. At most borders there may be check points on the roads but go a few hundred meters either side there is usually nothing, maybe a fence. So, if you are using a road get off it a few hundred meters before the border, skirt around the check point, and rejoin the road a few hundred yards on the other side. When crossing the border do so quickly, quietly and use all your senses and be alert for any patrols or remote cameras etc.

• Try to have or get maps, even free tourist guides are better than nothing.

• Learn to identify north and south without a compass.

• Always carry and try to conceal an escape compass on your person.

• Identify and remember prominent objects in the area such as major roads, rivers, mountains, airports and buildings, these will give you reference points when on the move.

• If you are in a rural area and want to locate people follow rivers, most villages are located around water sources.

Escape And Evasion Equipment

The reason for escape and evasion equipment is to help you escape from captivity and stay alive for a limited amount of time. You should carry a minimum amount of non-descript equipment as discreetly as possible. Expensive, specialist, flashy military equipment will only draw attention to you, it will be taken away by your captors or during a search and could possibly label you as some spy or police etc. This is something you don't want as it could lead to you being detained, tortured and executed. This list is a guide to what would be useful for you to have on your person, pick the items you think you would be able to get hold of, conceal and are relevant to the situation you're in.

- **Survival blanket:** These are usually silver in color and can be used to provide warmth, shelter, collect water and for signaling.

- **Personal water filter:** There are many small water filters on the market that are easily carried in a shirt pocket etc.

- **String or thin wire:** This has various uses for example construction of shelters, re-closing cut wire fences, trip wires etc.

- **Wire saw:** These thin wire saws can be used to cut wood, plastic and soft metals. Always try to buy those made from multiple strands of flexible wire "commando wire saws". Beware of cheap imitations.

- **Small lock pick set:** Bogota pics, diamond/needle file and cuff shims are easy to conceal and inexpensive.

- **Hacksaw blade:** The blade should be broken into 2 to 3 inch pieces to make them more concealable, if possible the ends and backs of the blades can be sharpened.

- **Safety pins:** Various uses including first aid, mending clothing, building shelters and picking open hand-cuffs.

- **Razor blades:** Small and concealable multi-purpose blades.

- **Flint and steel/Matches:** Used for fire lighting to keep you warm or cause distractions.

- **Tinder:** Cotton wool or lint etc. used to help you light fires.

- **Hairnet and Condoms:** Used for carrying water, the condom goes in the hairnet to stop it from splitting.

- **Water purification tabs:** For purifying drinking water.

- **Compass:** Choose a small and concealable compass.

- **Whistle & Mirror:** Can be used for signaling and distractions.

- **Knife:** Choose a small concealable knife that won't be found and confiscated when your captured or that can get you arrested for carrying an illegal weapon. Neck knives are an option as many searchers do not check the neck or chest areas.

• **Flashlights:** Choose a small concealable flashlight, forget the expensive tactical lights, this can be used for light, signaling and distractions.

• **Tools:** There are many good multi-plier type tools on the market that are excellent pieces of kit for escape and evasion, but they will most probably be confiscated straight away if your arrested or kidnapped.

• **Food:** Try to conceal high calorie foods such as sweets, nuts and raisins etc.

• **Money:** Probably the most important piece of equipment you can carry. Choose small value notes of a well-known currency, water-proof them and conceal them.

Concealing Escape Kit

Most commercial escape and evasion / survival kits come in a plastic or metal container. This container can be used to drink from and if it's metal you can also boil water in it. The trouble with tins and containers are that they are easy to find during a body search and will be confiscated. You want to try and conceal your equipment in your clothing.

• **Jackets:** There are lots of places for you to hide equipment in jackets especially if they are lined. Wire saws, matches and money can be sewn into seams and draw cords etc. with larger equipment put into the lining. The lining itself can be used for tinder etc.

• **Travel Vests:** These have lots of places to conceal equipment but there is a good chance it will be confiscated. A tactical vest is also an indicator that you are in the security business and an FBI wannabe.

- **Shirts:** Sew money etc. into the seams.

- **Trousers:** Sew money, wire saws, razor blades etc. in the waistband, hems and seams. Also keep a few bits of candy in your pockets.

- **Belts:** Sew equipment into your belt or look at buying a commercial money belt.

- **Shoes:** There is a lot of room to hide all sorts of equipment in the heels and soles of your shoes.

- **Underwear:** Sew money, wire saws etc. into the seams.

Always dress down and don't wear clothes that will draw attention to you or that will be taken off you by your captors. Again, this is just a guide to get you thinking, just take a few of the above-mentioned items, conceal them on your person as they could make your life a lot easier in an escape and evasion situation.

Camouflage & Concealment

It makes me laugh when I see a lot of SWAT Teams and PSD guys wearing Tactical Black and other colors that look cool but do nothing but make them stand out. In reality black is one of the worse colors to wear, what is black in nature, look around you and what in your surrounding's are black? I expect very little... In urban areas most walls are white, gray or cream... Light colors! The colors you wear should blend in with your background whether its day or night.

At night dark colors stand out, especially when moving past light backgrounds and in urban areas most backgrounds are light colors. Even in rural dry areas when moving through low bush and fields, the silhouettes of people in dark colors are easy to see at a distance.

You do not have to have expensive camouflage patterns to give you good concealment, a gray dress shirt and a pair of light khaki pants is way more effective than tactical Tim dressed in SWAT black!

Movement And Rural Camouflage

Modern humans are at a positive disadvantage when surviving and moving on foot in rural and wilderness areas. Most people these days have never spent a night outside without any cover, let alone in bad weather. When you're in the woods or bush you need to get comfortable in the environment. I remember one of my military instructors telling me that to be able to fight in an environment you must first be able to live comfortably in that environment, and this is very true. If you're having difficulty living day to day, then how can you operate effectively.

You need to start using all your senses as the animals do, and learn to identify sounds, smells, movements and what they mean. You need to especially be able to identify things associated with people, like footprints, cigarette stumps, broken twigs or foliage, fences, straight lines, domestic animals, aircraft, vehicles, talking etc. Think about human smells like fires, food, fuel, human waste and tobacco; if your senses are sharp in bush or wooded areas, then you should be able to smell or hear people before you see them. When moving you must do so quietly and regularly stop to look, listen and smell for any indication of people. If you identify people in your proximity, are you going to take cover, evade or ambush them?

You should always consider camouflage and wear clothes that blend in with your environment, in urban areas wear light blues and grays, and in rural areas browns and greens. As I have said before there is no need for military camouflage clothing as this will just draw attention to yourself.

Basic Field Craft

Things are seen because of these reasons: Shape, Shadow, Silhouette, Shine, Spacing & Movement.

• **Shape:** Disguise you're shape; use foliage or rags to break up your outline.

• **Shadow:** Keep in the shadows and always be aware that you are not casting a shadow that could be seen by your opposition.

• **Silhouette:** Don't stand out against skylines, lights, white walls, etc.

• **Shine:** No chrome, shiny watches, mirrored glasses, sparkly jewelry and the like.

• **Spacing:** If moving with others, remain spread out, but not too regularly and do not bunch together.

• **Movement:** Move carefully, a sudden movement draws attention and is the main reason camouflaged personnel and animals are seen.

The Basic Guidelines For Camouflage Are

• Learn to blend in with your surroundings.

• If you are using foliage to conceal yourself or your position don't use too much or too little.

• If you are in a long-term hide, remember to keep your camouflage fresh, dead foliage will alert people to your position.

• When moving avoid skylines.

• Don't use isolated or obvious cover; it's the first-place others will look. Consider hiding in thorny bushes or nettles as most people will not expect anyone to hide there.

• Camouflage your face, neck and any areas of the exposed flesh with mud, ash or charcoal from fires. Or use a balaclava or scarf to cover your face and wear gloves.

• Take all noisy objects from your pockets, such as keys and coins and make sure nothing on your person rattles.

• Make sure there are no shiny surfaces on your person, equipment or clothing.

Guidelines For Movement

You should always move quietly and cautiously to avoid stepping on dry twigs or breaking through foliage and undergrowth, as this will make noise and leave an easy trail to follow. If you know you're going to a rural area or possibly going to be in an escape and evasion situation avoid smelly foods, strong soaps and after shaves, as these will be easy to smell by those used to being in the bush. Always be careful not to leave signs you were in an area such as footprints, broken foliage, human waste or trash. Trash and human waste should be carried out of a hostile area and disposed of when safe to do so.

You should always move in "bounds" from one piece of cover to another. Your bounds should never be more than, say 50 yards, especially at night. When you stop at the end of each bound you should use your senses to try to detect any human presents then plan your next bound. Moving in short bounds is the safest way to move through populated areas or places there are unfriendly forces. Remember, always be prepared to take evasive action or to defend yourself.

The speed at which you travel will depend on whether it's day or night, the type of terrain you're in, and the number of people or terrorist / police patrols in the area. Never push yourself to your limit, you always need to have energy in reserve, so you can run in an emergency; tired people are also rarely mentally alert. If you must run from your opposition, try to do so only for a maximum of a few hundred yards, then slow down and move quietly, cautiously and cover any signs of your direction of travel. Do not use obvious routes, which tend to be the easiest routes to use; head up hills and into thorny areas etc.

There are no set time periods for halts, but you should try to take ten minutes in every hour on long journeys. Tracks, paths and roads make for fast, easy travel and can aid navigation but can also be very dangerous as your opponents will watch them closely. To be cautious walk a few meters off to the side of any roads or tracks. Places to expect sentries are at the entrances to urban areas, on bridges, crossroads and on high prominent terrain.

Avoid being silhouetted when crossing skylines and hills, go around them rather than over them where possible. If you need to cross an obstacle or skyline then keep low and crawl, if it's a fence, crawl through it or under it. If you have to cut through a fence, cut through the lower strands and then disguise the hole with undergrowth or tie the wire strands back together. Never cut through the top strands of a fence as this will be easily noticed.

Moving At Night

You need to learn to treat the night and darkness as your friend, darkness affords you cover. Many people are afraid of being in the dark, especially in rural areas or derelict buildings; you should use this to your advantage. If you are moving you should always try to stay in the shadows, if you get caught in a beam of light or car headlights you should freeze, the chances are that you will remain unnoticed. You must have your immediate reaction drills for encountering a person, being caught in light or hostile fire at the forefront of your mind. Being caught off guard will get you captured or killed.

There are both natural and manmade noises that are useful to you because they can cover up or disguise the sounds that you make when moving. The best time for moving covertly is during bad weather; rain will cover the noise of your movement and any ground sign you leave. Bad weather also keeps people under cover, and lowers the morale of those standing guard, learn to love bad weather.

General Guidelines For Rural Movement

• Wear clothing that blends in with local people and the terrain.

• Do everything possible to disguise evidence of your passage; cover footprints, never break twigs or undergrowth and repair broken foliage.

• Avoid contact with all people unless absolutely necessary.

• Litter, food and human waste must be buried or carried with you.

• Learn about tracking, then you'll be aware of what anyone following you will be looking for.

• If moving with others spread out and when crossing obstacles such as rivers or roads etc. take up positions to be able to give warnings of any threats that might be approaching. Also stay low, move fast, and cross one by one.

• Always be ready to take cover from gunfire or people you may encounter by surprise.

• Remember certain smells indicate human activity; odors float downhill in cool air and rise on warm air.

• Watch for stones, leaves or logs that have been moved, the undersides of these will be darker in color in damp environments, this can be an indicator of human activity or the location of hides.

• Always look for straight lines as they are rare in nature and are usually man made.

• Learn to identify unnatural vegetation, such as green leaves among dead branches or areas of too much foliage as this could indicate human activity, such as hides or ambushes.

These are some basic guidelines to get you thinking. These field skills can't be learnt while sat in a comfy chair, you need to get out and learn and practice them. Everything I have written about here is simple and the main thing required is situational awareness and common sense!

ORLANDO "ANDY" WILSON

Orlando has worked internationally at all levels of the specialist security and investigation industry for over 35 years. Over the years, he has become accustomed to the types of complications that can occur, when dealing with international law enforcement agencies and the problem of dealing with kidnapping, organized crime and Mafia groups.

His experience in the international security business began in 1988 when he enlisted in the British army at 17 years of age and volunteered for a 22-month frontline, operational tour in Northern Ireland in an Infantry unit, 4 Platoon, 1 WFR. He then joined his unit's Reconnaissance Platoon, with which he undertook intensive training in small-unit warfare.

Since leaving the British army in 1993, his time spent working in Eastern Europe in the 1990s gave him firsthand experience of the operational procedures of organized criminals and Mafia groups from the former Soviet Union. In addition, he had the opportunity to oversee criminal cases that have been the first of their kind in their respective country. His operations in Mexico training tactical police teams put him in a unique position to understand the war on Narco-Terrorism.

His continuous and ongoing projects focusing on kidnap and ransom prevention in South America, the Caribbean and West Africa have given him the knowledge to formulate practical programs to counter the kidnapping threat.

Orlando is a published author, writer, photographer and has been interviewed by numerous international TV and media outlets on topics ranging from kidnapping, organized crime to maritime piracy. He had his first article published in 1997 in an association magazine and his first book in 2012. He has been interviewed by media outlets ranging from the Professional Mariner Magazine, Newsweek Serbia, Newsweek en Espanol, GrupoMilenio, Mundo-Fox, The New York Times, the BBC, Soldier of Fortune Magazine and others.

Orlando's diverse and continuous operational experience enables him to provide no-nonsense professional services and training programs. His operational investigation and close protection procedures are cutting edge and the most effective commercially available. He is also a founding member and operations manager of Risks Incorporated.

OTHER BOOKS BY ORLANDO

These Books are Available on Amazon!

Non-Fiction Manuals

• Social Navigation: A Practical Survival Guide for Human Interactions

• Counter Insurgency Operations: A tactical Guide for Law Enforcement

• Intelligence Gathering: Front Line HUMINT Considerations

• Caribbean Security Threats: A threat assessment for the islands of the Caribbean

• Gun Range Management: A Guide for Range Managers, Range Safety Officers & Firearms Instructors

• Investigative Journalist Security: Staying Alive to Tell the Truth

• Threat Assessments for Close Protection & Security Management

• Protecting Your Loved Ones: Security Awareness for Parents & Adults

• Close Protection: Luxury & Hostile Environments

• Close Protection & Firearms

• The Close Protection Business

• Home & Office Security: Protection of Residencies & Businesses

• Travel Security: Personal Travel & Vehicle Security

• Counter Terrorism: Terrorist Attack Response

• Kidnap & Ransom: The Essentials of Kidnapping Prevention

• Shoot First & Shoot Last: The Real-World Guide to Pistol Craft

Crime Fiction

• The Shoot: An Assassin's World

• Vengeance: The Art of Pain

• The Collectors: Death is Easy, Life is Hard

• Reglas Mexicanas: A Life Without Pain, Is Not A Life

Photo Books

• Athens Lockdown 2020 in Pictures

• Wandering in Serbia

• Vigilantes of Imo – Nigerian Vigilante Life in Pictures